MAKING
CLOTHES
for Children

MAKING CLOTHES
for Children

BETTY FOSTER

Macdonald

A Macdonald BOOK

Text and patterns © Betty Foster 1985
Illustrations and design © Macdonald & Co (Publishers) Ltd 1985
Photographs © Fiona Pragoff 1985

First published in Great Britain in 1985
by Macdonald & Co (Publishers) Ltd
London & Sydney

A member of BPCC plc

British Library Cataloguing in Publication Data

Foster, Betty
    Making clothes for children.
    1. Children's clothing
    I. Title
    646.4'06   TT635

    ISBN 0-356-10845-7

Filmset by Flair plan phototypesetting Ltd.
Printed and bound in Great Britain by
Purnell and Sons (Book Production) Ltd, Paulton, Bristol.

Clothes design Anni Bankhead
Book design Sally Downes
Photographer Fiona Pragoff
Assistant Christine Withroe
**Styling, make-up and
hairdressing** Jackie Batten
Additional hairdressing Jane
Hearne, Lorraine O'Riordan, Ann
Homewood
Illustrations Ron Hayward
(patterns), Jil Shipley (sewing
techniques), Clare Forte (motifs)
Fabrics John Lewis Partnership,
Liberty, Laura Ashley
Shoes Clarks

Macdonald & Co (Publishers) Ltd
Maxwell House
74 Worship Street
London EC2A 2EN

Contents

Acknowledgements

The publishers would like to thank Mr Lothian and
the children of St George's Primary School, London
W1 who appear in this book: Danielle Emerton, Paul
Emerton, Ingrid Gardner, Rachel Gardner, Justin
Green, Paul Hardcastle, Richard Jarrett, Takaki
Kikuchi, Sarah Liew, Karen Manley, Jennifer
McLauchlan, Anne Murrell, Rupal Somani and
Angelique Stephenson. Many thanks also to Navlett
Bent, Joanna Burgess and Dena O'Hara.

Special thanks to the following companies for their
generous help: Benetton, The Button Box, Clarks
Shoes, Honda (UK) Ltd, John Lewis Partnership,
Liberty and Mothercare.

Introduction

Over the years I have heard many women say, 'I would love to make clothes for children, but I have trouble with the fitting, and the sewing is so complicated that the child has grown out of the garment before I have finished the making'. Add to this the price of buying patterns as the children grow (and they do not grow in regular proportions, like blowing up a balloon) and you find that you are in one of the most complicated areas of dressmaking. So what can be done about it?

Sewing

The sewing techniques must be simple and quick, so that you are not trying to learn too many complicated methods too quickly. It's rather like cookery, where you rapidly learn the basic ingredients of a sponge cake, and then build up confidence to make decisions about adding currants, flavourings and fancy icing as your taste (or fashion) changes.

The sewing techniques necessary to make the garments in this book are illustrated at the back on pages 106–146. You should familiarize yourself with these 'ingredients' *before* you start sewing.

Patterns

All children are individual and their clothes size can rarely be judged by age. For example, a three-year-old and an eleven-year-old might both need garments in the size range for seven-year-olds. The *only* sure way to determine size is to take a few simple measurements of your child, choose the nearest matching Base Size and then refine it to fit your particular child.

Three Base Size bodices and sleeves are given on pages 14–15. When you have taken the measurements and consulted the comparison charts I would strongly advise you to make up a bodice and sleeve in cheap fabric:

a To ensure you have chosen the correct base size.

b To recognize the 'refinements' that all the patterns in the book will require to personalize them to your child.

Measuring your child

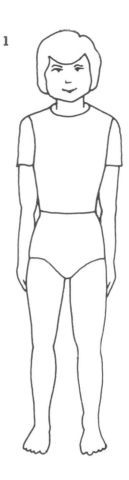

All the measurements in this book are given in *centimetres* so measure your child in centimetres. If you prefer to measure in inches you should buy an analogical tape measure, which is marked in both inches and centimetres so you can convert quickly.

The child to be measured should wear a T-shirt and pants. Jumpers and shirts tucked into skirts and trousers will not give a good result. Do not measure too tightly; it is better to err on the slack side because none of the garments involves critical fitting that demands rigid accuracy with the tape measure.

1 Tie a piece of tape or string quite tightly round the waist, much tighter than the child would wear a belt, so that it settles in the natural waistline just above the pelvis. If you say, 'My child hasn't got a waist' then you must decide where you would like this position to be and fix the tape there.

2 With arms by the side, measure the shoulder width by imagining a ruler held across the highest part of the back.

3 Measure the centre back bodice length from the base of the neck to the tape tied around the waist.

4 Measure around the chest just below the armpit at nipple level. **Note** This should be the biggest body circumference measurement.

5 Measure the waist at the position where the tape is tied. (DO NOT measure as tightly as the tape.)

6 Measure the biggest hip circumference by holding the tape around the body about 10 cm below the waist, and then sliding it downwards until you find the biggest measurement.

7 Measure the arm length from the point where you took the shoulder width to the wrist. Do this with the elbow bent.

8 Measure around the top arm. You will find this measurement useful for elastication and for the cuffs on puffed sleeves.

9 Measure the skirt length from the waist tape to the level required. This will vary as fashion changes.

10 Measure the crutch length from the centre back waist, through the legs to the centre front waist. Use the waist tape as the guide for waist position.

11 Measure the inside leg length to just below the ankle bone.

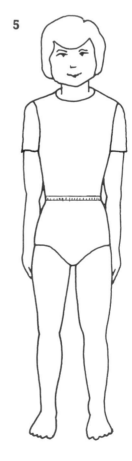

Waist =

2

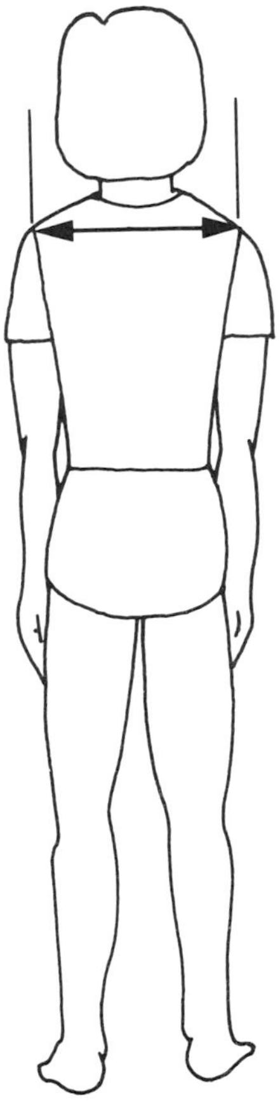

Shoulder width =

3

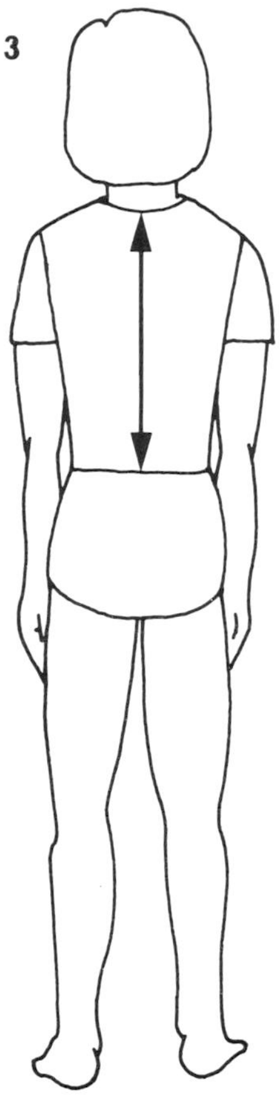

CB bodice length =

4

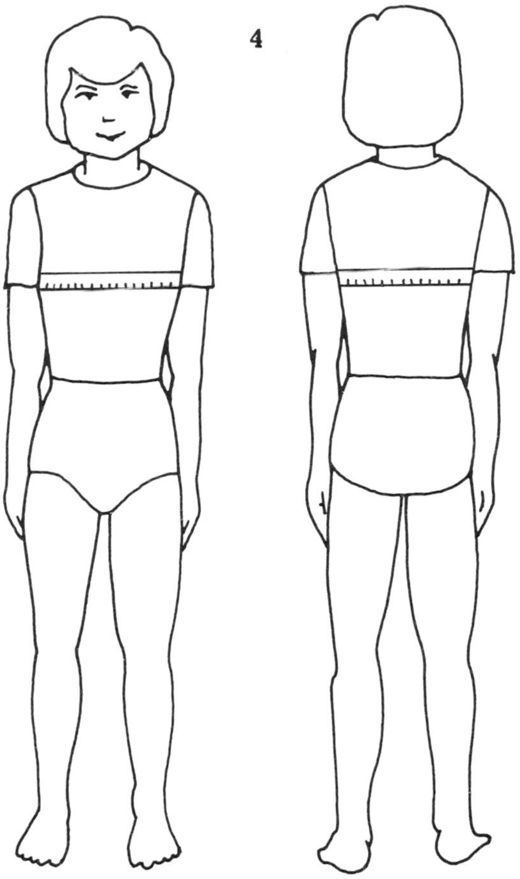

Chest measurement =

6

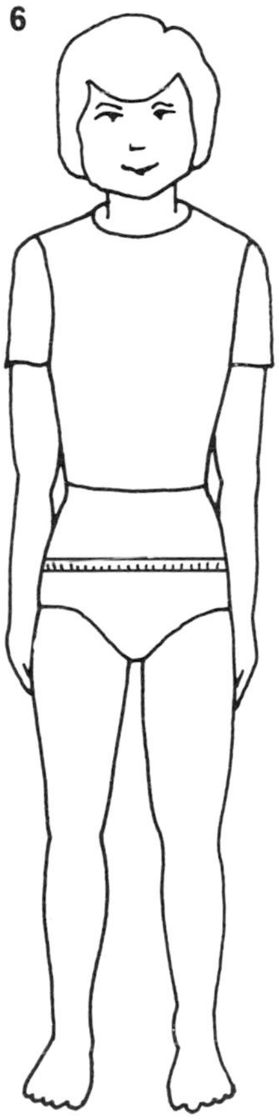

Biggest hip =

7

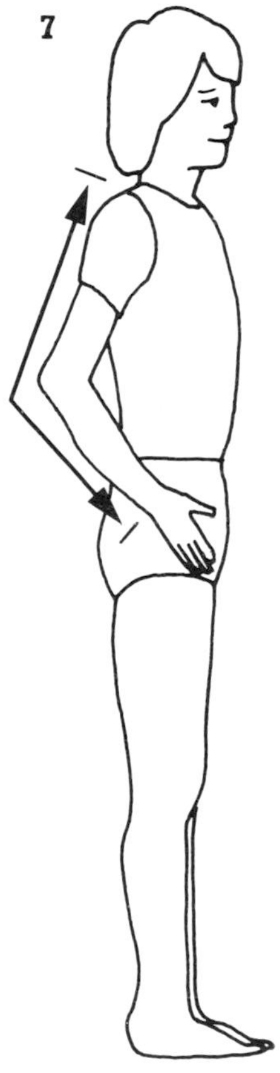

Sleeve length =

8

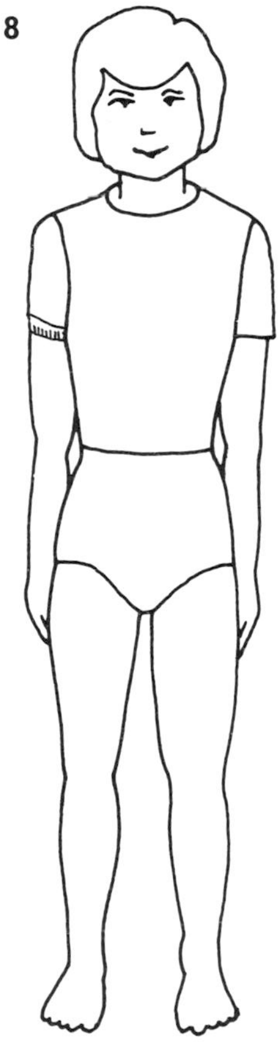

Top arm =

9

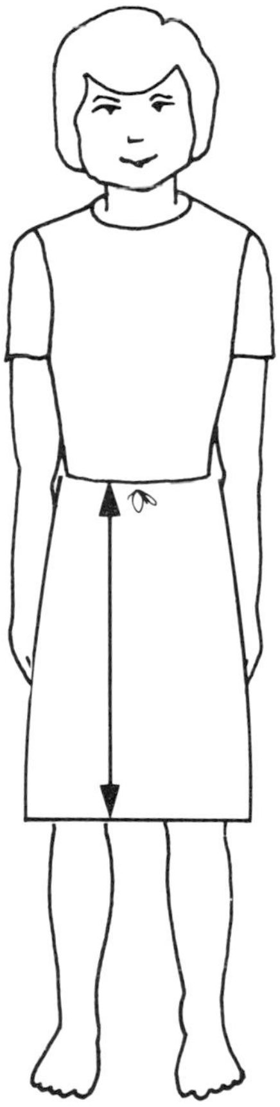

Skirt length =

10

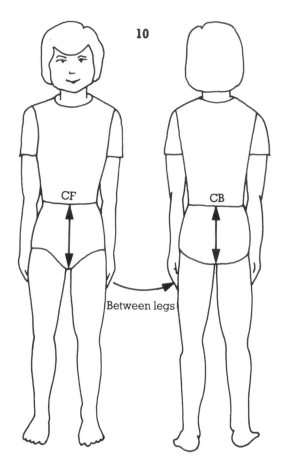

CF

CB

Between legs

Crutch measurement =

11

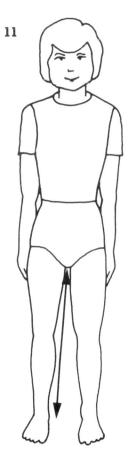

Inside leg =

Making a pattern

The success of your sewing will depend mainly upon getting the bodice and waistline correct. It is then a simple matter to attach skirts and trousers.

To help you achieve a good fit, basic bodice patterns are shown on pages 14-15, and you should use them in conjunction with your child's measurements as explained below. If you happen to select the wrong starting pattern it is far better to get it too big rather than too small. You then have the option of either taking in the garment or knowing that your child will grow into it eventually.

Note All the patterns in this book are illustrated on a squared grid, each square representing 4 cm.

How to start

Fill in your child's measurements on the chart here and then turn to the Basic Bodice Block charts and and diagrams on pages 13 and 14.

1 Look first at the centre back length options, and compare your child's centre back length with those offered. Would lengthening the bodice front and back be the only adjustment needed for your child?

2 Consider the chest size-ranges offered. Which base pattern is closest in size to your child?

3 Assess the shoulder widths offered. Are you able to widen or narrow this measurement within the limitations illustrated?

The comparison of these three measurements and the alternatives presented in the Basic Bodice Block should allow you to judge which of the three you will find most successful as a starting point.

Measurement chart

DATE

NAME

Shoulder width:

Centre back bodice length:

Chest measurement:

Waist measurement:

Biggest hip measurement:

Arm (sleeve) length:

Top arm:

Skirt length:

Crutch measurement:

Inside leg:

Base patterns

The three basic bodice blocks and sleeve blocks illustrated on pages 14-16 indicate the Base Sizes of three age groups, each represented by a different grading line.

- The solid line in each case illustrates the Base Pattern outline for the following age groups: 3-4, 5-7 and 9-10.
- The broken line (_ _ _ _) illustrates how the Base Pattern can be *reduced* within the recommended limits.
- The dotted line (. . . .) illustrates how the Base Pattern can be *increased* within the recommended limits.

The patterns in the book are drawn to the Base Size and can be increased or decreased in shoulder width, chest circumference and bodice length by using the methods described in the Base Pattern instruction.

For each pattern the Base Size is written in brackets: (3-4), (5-6-7), (9-10). The ages outside the brackets indicate the range to which increasing or decreasing should prove satisfactory: 2(3-4)5, 4(5-6-7)8, 8(9-10)11. It must be stressed that these ages are only an indication of which Base Pattern could be right for your child. However, as age and size rarely coincide in children, it is vital that you follow the instructions to establish the best starting point for *your child's* patterns.

	Your Child	Nearest Base Size	(Plus) or (Minus) Alteration
Shoulder Width			
Chest			
Centre Back Length			

CHEST ALTERATION LIMITS

DOTTED LINE	INCREASE
Add 0.5 cm	Increases chest 2 cm
Add 1 cm	Increases chest 4 cm
BROKEN LINE	DECREASE
Reduce 0.5 cm	Decreases chest 2 cm
Reduce 1 cm	Decreases chest 4 cm

AGE SIZE RANGE	Limit of decrease	BASE SIZE 3-4	Limit of increase	Limit of decrease	BASE SIZE 5-7	Limit of increase	Limit of decrease	BASE SIZE 9-10	Limit of increase
SHOULDER WIDTH (in cm)	19	21	23	24	26	28	27	29	31
TO FIT CHEST (in cm)	50-53	54	55-58	55-58	59	60-63	66-69	70	71-74
CENTRE BACK BODICE LENGTH (in cm)	23 Lengthen or shorten front and back at waist up to 4 cm.			27 Lengthen or shorten front and back at waist up to 4 cm.			33 Lengthen or shorten front and back at waist up to 4 cm.		

ALTERATIONS

Any alterations made to the side seams of the bodice must also be made to the sleeve seams. You must select the same size sleeve block to go with your chosen bodice block.

SLEEVE LENGTH

	PATTERN	YOUR CHILD	PLUS OR MINUS
Base 3-4	33 cm		
Base 3-7	42 cm		
Base 9-10	48 cm		

Lengthen or shorten at bottom of sleeve

Personalizing the pattern

Once you have chosen the most likely starting point, and do remember that the age of your child is no guide to what this will be, you should write your child's measurements on the chart on page 13.

Bodices

1 Compare the details of your child against the Basic Bodice Block and make a note of any adjustments necessary to fit your child. The following adjustments are possible:

a Widening and narrowing of shoulders.
b Taking in or letting out of side seams to increase or decrease the waist and chest measurement.
c Lengthening the bodice front and back, within the recommended limit of 4 cm either longer or shorter.

2 Make the pattern of your selected base bodice and adjust it to your child's measurements.

Basic bodice blocks

RECTANGLE 44 x 28 cm

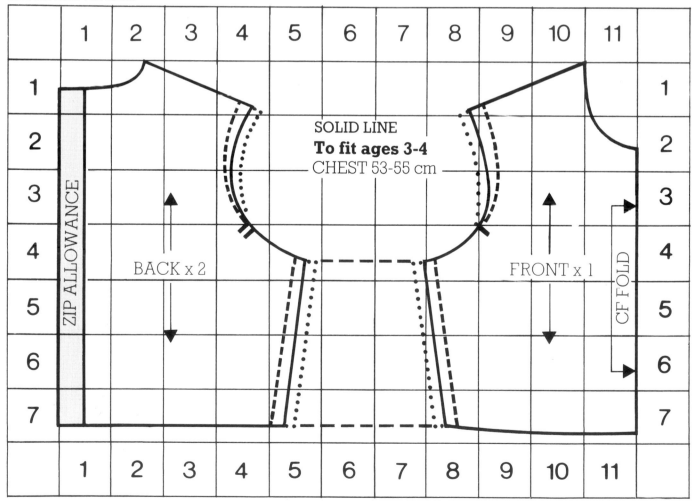

SOLID LINE
To fit ages 3-4
CHEST 53-55 cm

ZIP ALLOWANCE

BACK x 2

FRONT x 1

CF FOLD

RECTANGLE 44 x 36 cm

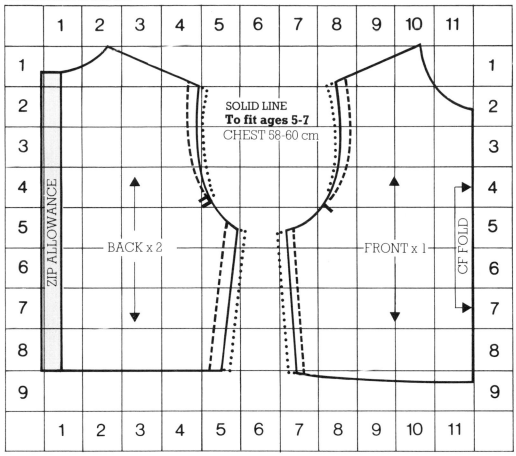

	1	2	3	4	5	6	7	8	9	10	11	

SOLID LINE
To fit ages 5-7
CHEST 58-60 cm

ZIP ALLOWANCE

BACK x 2

FRONT x 1

CF FOLD

RECTANGLE 48 x 40 cm

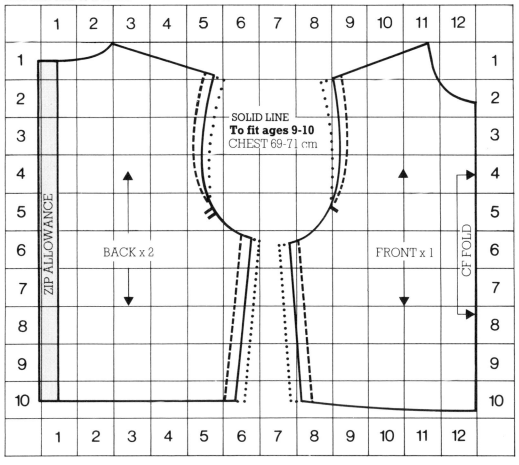

	1	2	3	4	5	6	7	8	9	10	11	12	

SOLID LINE
To fit ages 9-10
CHEST 69-71 cm

ZIP ALLOWANCE

BACK x 2

FRONT x 1

CF FOLD

Sleeves

1 For accurate checking you must use a Basic Sleeve the same size as your chosen Basic Bodice.

2 The top of the sleeve has a definite relationship with the armhole, so if you have increased or decreased the side seams of the bodice you must do the same with the sleeve seams.

3 The sleeve pattern length should be checked, from the top centre of the sleeve to the stitching line at the wrist.

Increasing the length Add the required amount at the wrist.

Shortening the length Fold the pattern across about half way down the side seam and pleat out the required amount.

Basic sleeve blocks

SOLID LINE

To fit ages 3-4

RECTANGLE 32 x 36 cm

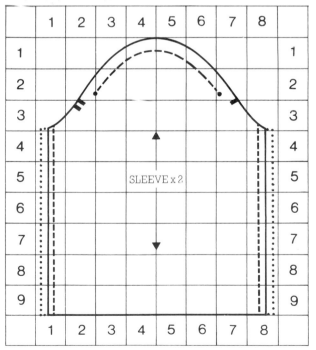

SOLID LINE

To fit ages 5-7

RECTANGLE 36 x 44 cm

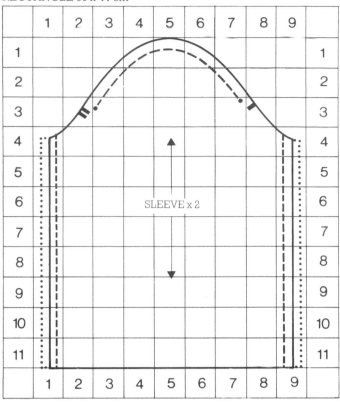

SOLID LINE

To fit ages 9-10

RECTANGLE 48 x 52 cm

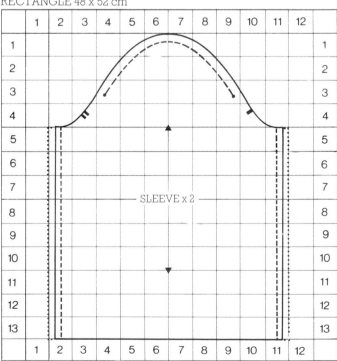

Skirts

Apart from the school skirt on page 66, none of the garments in the book has a critical hip fitting. As gathers are used on all other waists and yoke-lines, you have only to keep track of the length as your child grows.

1 Check the length of skirt required, remembering to add a 1.5 cm top seam allowance and a 5 cm hem, before lengthening or shortening the skirt at the hem line. You must do this to the pattern *before cutting out the fabric.*

2 For dresses without a defined waist you should add the centre back bodice length to the skirt length, then check your pattern from the centre back neck to the bottom of the hem.

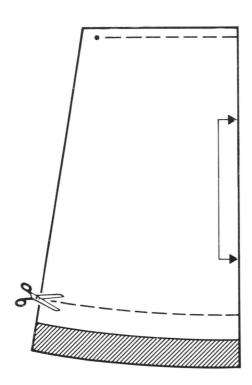

Trousers

Four measurements are involved in trousers:

- Waist size (elasticated in our pattern so not critical)
- Hip size (not critical because of the elasticated waist, but must be watched)
- Crutch measurement (varies from person to person)
- Inside leg measurement (when used in conjunction with a measured crutch length it gives an accurate trouser length)

How to make your trouser pattern

1 Copy your child's nearest size pattern from the diagrams on page 50.

2 Draw 'grading' lines on the front and back pattern pieces as illustrated below.

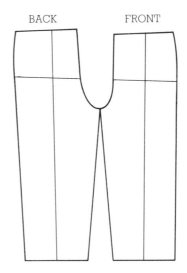

3 Cut the front and back patterns into four pieces so that you can manipulate them into the correct hip size, crutch length and inside leg length as your child grows.

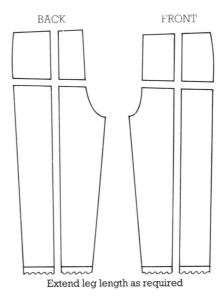

Extend leg length as required

Conclusions

All the patterns in this book have been made from the four starting Base Patterns that you have been studying.

You now know how each pattern needs 'refining' to make it specially for your child. When you copy the patterns in this book you must always refer to your child's measurements (noted on page 11) and make the appropriate adjustments. However, as children grow so quickly and erratically, you should always be prepared to remeasure them *before making any pattern,* as you have the information to 'grow' the patterns or change the starting base if you find it necessary.

Sizing patterns

If you took off the clothes you are wearing and measured them, you would be quite shocked to discover that they are actually a great deal bigger than your body measurements. The labels in clothes, and the instructions on patterns say quite clearly 'This garment is to fit size 00'. They do *not* say 'This garment measures 00'.

The reason for the difference between body and garment measurements is that ready-made clothes and patterns used in dressmaking have two types of *ease* added to the body measurements they are intended to fit.

Fitting ease

In order to get a garment on (unless it is very stretchy) it must measure at least 4 – 5 cm more than the body on all the circumference measurements. This will give quite a close fitting garment.

Fitting ease is included in all the diagram patterns.

Fashion and styling ease

In order to create a particular 'look', designers add fashion ease to their garments, the amount added varying from designer to designer and pattern to pattern. If you make a good base pattern of your child you can use it as a template to assess and correct the ease on any other patterns you may buy. This will allow you to make adjustments *before cutting out* if you think it necessary.

All the patterns in this book have fitting and fashion ease included in the diagrams. When adjusting shoulder width, side seams, sleeve seams and body or skirt length for your child *do not add any further fitting or fashion ease.*

The 'oversized look' is very popular and can easily be achieved by making the garment a size bigger than usual. This is very useful for children who can then grow into a closer fit.

How to use the patterns

Before you copy your first pattern from the book you must decide which size range is going to give the best possible starting point for your child.

Copying the patterns

The patterns are illustrated on a squared grid, each square representing 4 cm. You will need to prepare rectangles of paper in the sizes stated and divide them into 4 cm squares ready to copy from the book diagrams.

The paper

You can buy centimetre squared paper from stationers and office equipment shops, or Betty Foster's dressmaking paper ready printed with 4 cm squares, from haberdashery shops or by mail order from P.O. Box 28, Crewe.

However, you don't have to spend money on special paper. You can use newspaper, ceiling lining paper or any sheets cut to the correct rectangle size. The paper must be divided into 4 cm squares ready for copying the patterns.

Method 1
Cut rectangles of paper to the sizes indicated on the pattern, then use a ruler or tape measure to mark 4 cm spaces along the edges as shown below.

Draw lines to form the squares, using a pencil and ruler.

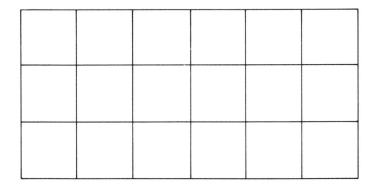

Method 2
Cut rectangles of paper to the sizes indicated in the pattern, then carefully fold a strip 4 cm wide down one edge. Continue folding concertina fashion to the opposite edge. Press the creases sharply into place.

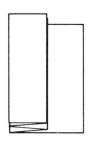

Repeat the procedure from the remaining edge so that your paper is creased into squares.

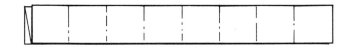

You can either draw lines on the folds or use the crease lines as your grid.

Marking up

Number the squares across the top and down the sides of your paper. **Note** If you make your own grid paper rather than using purchased paper, the numbered squares *are part of the rectangle size,* not additional to it as shown in the book. Mark the points you are copying from the diagrams on each square. Finally, join up the points you have marked using a ruler for straight lines, and a flexible curved ruler (available from office suppliers) for drawing the curves.

Pattern information

It is very important to transfer all pattern markings from the diagrams on to the full size pattern. These are indicated below.

In the book

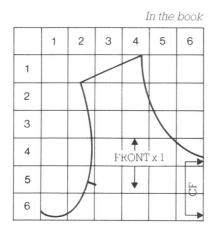

Copied on 4 cm squares

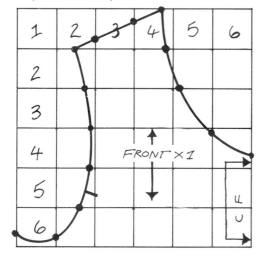

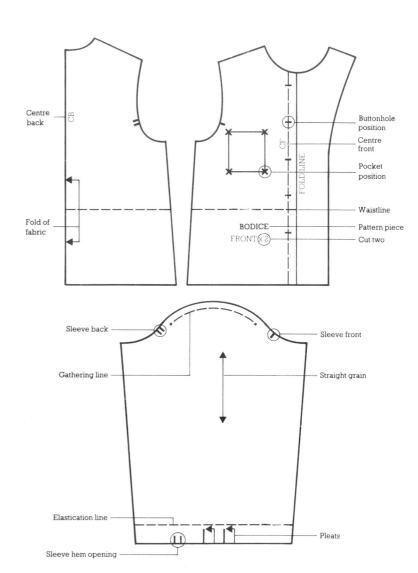

Successful sewing

What equipment do you need?

It is not necessary to have a sophisticated sewing machine to make acceptable garments that will keep you and your family fashionably dressed in well-made clothes. Many people enjoy sewing small children's clothes by hand, using the same sewing techniques and procedures as if a sewing machine were available. For this reason, virtually all the sewing instructions in the Order of making for each garment in the book say 'stitch'; the method is for you to choose.

Sewing machines

If you have a sewing machine you will need a good forward and reverse stitch facility. A swing-needle zig-zag stitch is also a tremendous help for making buttonholes, decorating edges and finishing seams. It can be set very small to give some stretch to seams, which is particularly useful on stretch fabrics used for sportswear. These call for seams that stretch as much as the fabric, and there are many machines now available that have special stretch stitches designed for these modern fabrics.

Never underestimate the value of old hand machines; they can be an excellent introduction to dressmaking. If, however, you decide to invest in a new machine, do look at a good selection and try to see them demonstrated on a variety of different fabrics before you commit yourself to buying.

Sewing thread

This plays an important part in successful dressmaking. It must be of good quality and colourfast when washed. I strongly recommend that you buy only 'branded' makes, which are well tested and researched by the manufacturers.

Sewing needles

Reliable brands of needle are essential. A variety of special needles are available to deal with modern fabrics that can be difficult to handle. Ask about them at a good haberdashery counter.

Pins

You will use pinning in place of tacking, as well as for fastening pattern pieces to fabric before cutting out. Ensure that the pins are stainless steel and do not leave them in the garment for longer than necessary. A magnetic pin box (available from office suppliers) can be the dressmaker's best friend.

Scissors

Good cutting-out scissors are an investment and should be bought, like a tennis racket, by trying them and weighing them in your hands to make sure they are comfortable for you personally. Small, sharp embroidery scissors can be used for trimming and cutting buttonholes, and also for unpicking, should you find it necessary.

How much fabric do you need?

This book does not give the amount of fabric required for the garments for two very good reasons:

1 I do not know the size of your child.

2 I do not know the width of the fabric you are going to choose.

So much fabric is wasted by giving estimates of the amount you might require that I prefer to give information on how to calculate your requirements much more accurately. It involves some once-only preparation work by you, but I think it well worth the time involved for the long-term savings that you will make.

Fabric widths

Fabric is available in the following widths:
- 90 cm
- 115 cm
- 135 cm
- 150 cm
- 175 cm

Cutting out from these widths is most often done with the fabric folded in half lengthways. You should make yourself *fabric planners* up to three metres long in each width. Use either a roll of paper or cheap fabric for each planner and mark it up as shown overleaf.

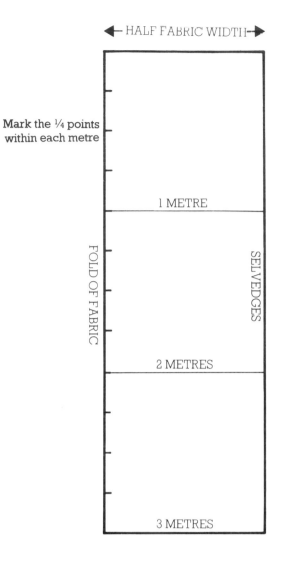

← HALF FABRIC WIDTH →

Mark the ¼ points
within each metre

FOLD OF FABRIC

SELVEDGES

1 METRE

2 METRES

3 METRES

When you have made and checked your patterns you can place them on the planner and read off the minimum length of fabric from which you could economically cut the garment.

I made my *fabric planners* over twenty years ago — in calico for the narrow widths and jersey for the wider widths — using a ballpoint pen to make the marks. They wash well and have given me accurate purchasing information for my fabric requirements ever since.

Cutting out

A firm, flat surface is ideal for cutting out. I know that many people use the floor, despite the difficulties that it presents, but a surface at working height is much more comfortable. I have made a cutting board from hardboard 1.5 metres long and 90 cm wide. On the rough side I have stuck down a piece of felt, which is a good surface to pin pattern pieces for checking, and it also acts as protection for my dining table when I turn it over to the smooth side to become my cutting table.

On the smooth side I have drawn lines to indicate the various fabric widths, other lines to give me accurate cross-way positioning, and various buttonhole distances. In this way it acts as a permanent memo board.

The advantage of this type of home-made cutting-out table is that I can swivel it round as I am working and thus avoid awkward pinning and cutting angles. It can be easily stored behind a wardrobe or under a single bed.

Additional requirements

Lining and interfacing should be discussed with the shop assistant when you buy your fabric. He or she can advise you on the appropriate weight and type to buy. Buttons and other fastenings, particularly zip fasteners, should be bought with the fabric.

There are many new and exciting sewing aids being produced to help make dressmaking easier. Try to spend some time browsing in shops and take advantage of anything that makes for quicker and more satisfying results.

Sewing techniques

There are many excellent books explaining how to sew, that have many different methods of dealing with the same problem. However, they can appear very intimidating, especially to the beginner, who could be led to believe that sewing is a difficult subject involving a lot of learning and a degree of perfection before it is possible to make anything worthwhile.

There are, in fact, surprisingly few sewing techniques that you have to learn in order to make highly successful clothes. The secret is to master the essential basic skills, which are:
● Seams
● Darts
● Zips
● Hems
● Gathering
● Facings
● Binding
You will find that these techniques are constantly needed and occur time and again in different patterns. You will add new skills to this basic repertoire as you make more and more garments.

When you have studied the illustrated sewing techniques on pages 106-146, choose a garment you would like to make and read through the order of making, ticking the techniques you know and understand. If you are a complete beginner you will not have many ticks, but do not be discouraged. Study and practise the techniques you need to know on small pieces of fabric. You will quickly be able to tick more methods as you make each garment and will only have to refer to the sewing technique section of the book when you find a process that you have not done before.

Note Never use a technique for the first time on a garment. Try it out first as a sample.

Summary

The contents of a book like this may look both exciting and daunting to a beginner. In order to help you, the *essential* points to which you must refer are summarized here.

1 Measure your child carefully and at regular intervals to keep track of his or her growth.

2 Always work with the nearest possible pattern size and adjust the fitting of the pattern *before* cutting out your fabric.

3 Choose fabric carefully, ensuring that your machine will be able to sew it well.

4 Fabric belts and sashes can usually be made from fabric left over after cutting out. This ensures that they will wash as well as the garment.

5 Practise the sewing techniques on scraps of fabric whenever you have a few spare minutes.

6 Always press a small piece of fabric before pressing any part of a garment to ensure that the iron is set to the correct temperature.

7 Never iron over pins or tacking in the garment.

8 Learn to recognize the pattern markings and instructions (illustrated on page 20).

9 Learn to recognize the various shadings used in the sewing techniques section on pages 106-146.

Right side is indicated by green.

Wrong side is indicated by white.

Interfacing (where recommended) is indicated by

Towelling Cape

Start sewing with something simple; a soft towel or piece of towelling fabric is all you need, plus some contrast crossway binding.

This cosy wrap is a semicircle of fabric with a radius of any size you care to select. The rounded corners make the binding much easier to attach. Start at the bottom centre point. (See sewing technique 1.)

I have used binding to match the bikini on page 45 as this cape could be a welcome beach accessory for an older child. Binding is a sewing technique used over and over again in dressmaking, particularly with children's clothes where it replaces the facings often used on bigger garments.

This garment can also be made with a hood. Select one of the hood diagrams from pages 34 or 42. Cut out and stitch the hood. Position it on centre point of straight edge of cape and stitch. The binding should be continued round the outer edge of the hood.

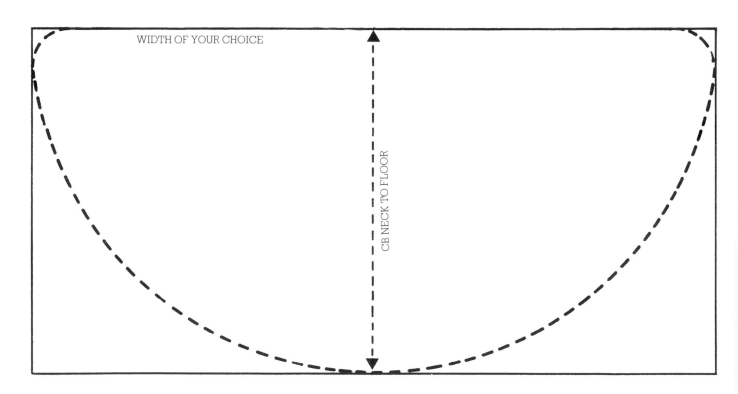

WIDTH OF YOUR CHOICE

CB NECK TO FLOOR

Baby's Bib

Shower curtaining, PVC or any washable fabric can be used to make this bib. Don't forget to check that your binding is washable and colourfast.

Order of making

(See sewing techniques 1 and 2.)

1 Bind top of pocket. Position it on bottom edge of bib and stitch round to hold it in place for binding.

2 Bind round all outer edges of bib *except neckline*.

3 Place point A to point A and point B to point B and stitch together to form sleeve.

4 Bind neckline, leaving long ends to tie behind neck.

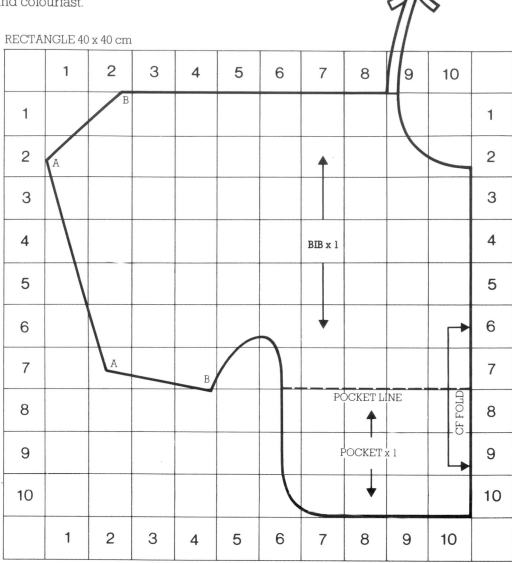

RECTANGLE 40 x 40 cm

BIB x 1

POCKET LINE

CF FOLD

POCKET x 1

Sleeping Bag

This is one of the easiest things to make for a baby and can be made from a wide variety of fabrics for winter and summer. The fleecy acrylic fabric we have used washes easily and keeps its colour well. The zip should also be colourfast, as should any motifs that you buy to trim the garment. When outgrown it can be unpicked across the bottom, hemmed and used as a toddler's dressing-gown.

The pattern gives a hood as an alternative to the collar used in the photograph.

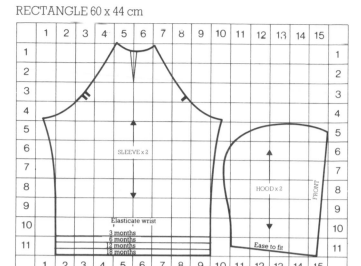

RECTANGLE 60 x 44 cm

Order of making

(See sewing techniques 2, 7, 13, 14 and 11.)

1 Stitch centre front seam from base of zip opening to bottom edge and insert zip.

2 Stitch back of sleeves to back of garment.
Stitch front of sleeves to front of garment.

3 Stitch sleeve seams and side seams in one operation.

4 Make and attach collar or hood.

5 From inside of bag, stitch across bottom edge.

6 Hem sleeves and insert elastic.

To fit ages 3-18 months
RECTANGLE 60 x 68 cm

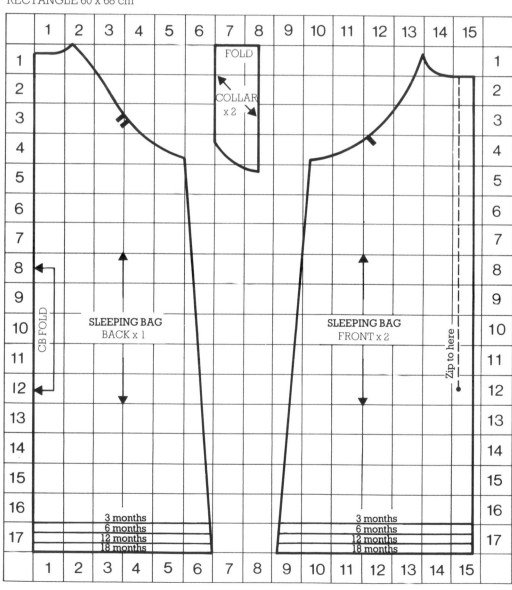

Rompers and Mob Cap

Rompers may be worn by both boys and girls, in many different fabrics: cotton and polyester for warm weather, denim, needlecord or jersey for winter wear. The straps are fixed in the seam at the front and buttoned to the required length at the back. There is no side seam in the pattern, although the position is indicated in case you want one.

Our garment has been made with a fine cotton lining, but you could use a Dicel taffeta or even a fine waterproof material. Boilproof elastic is recommended to allow for constant washing. For girls, you might like to make the matching mob cap.

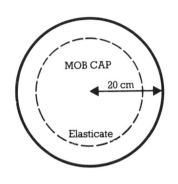

The mob cap

Order of making

1 Cut a circle of fabric 40 cm in diameter and tack a line 6 cm in from outer edge. Gather on this line until cap is about 10 cm bigger than child's head.

2 Stitch elastic on this line so that mob cap grips slightly. A lace trim can be added to the mob cap and romper legs.

Rompers

Order of making

(See sewing techniques 2, 23, 17, 6 and 18.)

Note The main fabric and the lining are made separately in exactly the same way up to point 3. They are then stitched together at the top edge. Make two separate legs, leaving the crutch seam until last.

1 Stitch side seams.

2 Stitch inside leg seams.

3 Stitch crutch seam. (This also forms the bibbed front.) Repeat steps 1 – 3 to make lining.

4 Make straps and stitch to main fabric at front position.

5 With right sides together place main fabric romper *inside* lining romper and stitch around top edge only.

6 Turn lining to inside of romper, then tack and stitch lining and main fabric together at bottom of each leg. Turn a small hem or decoratively neaten these edges.

To fit ages 18 months-2 years
RECTANGLE 48 x 40 cm

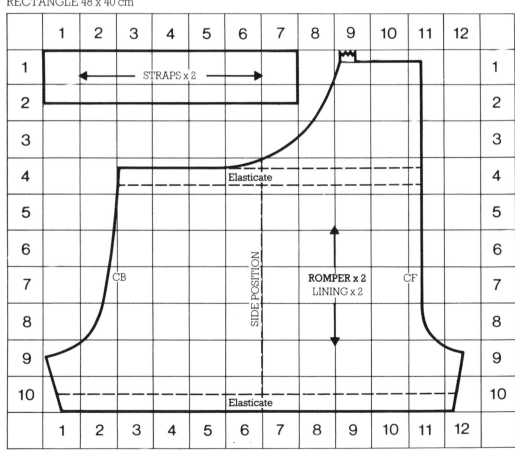

7 Stitch two rows of machining to carry elastic at waist. Stitch elastic into legs.

8 Check the cross-over strap length at the back and add buttons and buttonholes, or stitch into place.

Dungarees

With the bib top at back and front, and fixed strap length, these dungarees make excellent playwear. In the diagram pattern for 1 – 2 year-olds, the side seams have been drawn touching each other so that you can easily cut the garment *without* a side seam; simply pin the two pattern pieces together before cutting out. The legs can be elasticated if you prefer, but poppers on the inside leg seams are very useful for small children. Complete kits, with a tool to attach the poppers, can be bought in most large department stores. If you use a denim-type fabric, choose a soft one that will be easy to sew and comfortable to wear. If it has an attractive reverse side, you can use it to trim the garment as shown in the picture. The pockets are optional.

Order of making

(See sewing techniques 17, 15, 2, 16 and 4.)

1 Make straps and pockets. Prepare trim and stitch into position on relevant pieces.

2 Small sizes: Stitch side seam. Attach pockets. Stitch centre front and centre back seams. Leave crutch seam open for addition of popper fastenings.
Large sizes: Make two separate legs. Stitch side seams. Stitch inside leg seams. Stitch crutch seam. Stitch bib pocket to front.

3 Stitch centre front, centre back and side seams of facings.

4 Stitch straps to top back of garment.

5 Stitch facings to top edge, enclosing straps at back.

6 Stitch a casing to waistline on inside of dungarees and insert elastic as indicated in diagram.

7 Make buttonholes in front of garment and stitch buttons on straps.

Note If you make the straps long you can lengthen the garment as your child grows by repositioning the buttons.

8 Turn and stitch hems.

To fit ages 1-2
RECTANGLE 48 x 76 cm

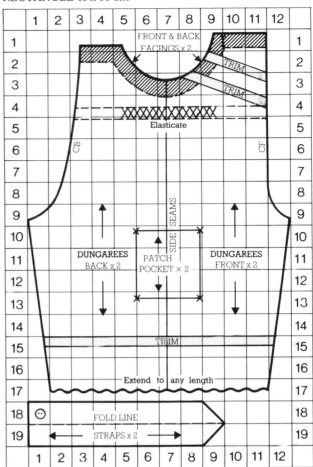

To fit ages 3-4
RECTANGLE 56 x 72 cm

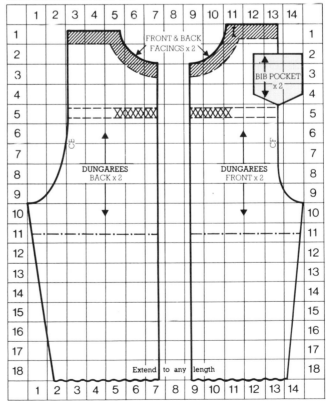

RECTANGLE 32 x 8 cm

	1	2	3	4	5	6	7	8	
1				FOLD LINE					1
2	⊙	←		STRAPS x 2			→		2
	1	2	3	4	5	6	7	8	

Pramsuit

This is a versatile pattern because it can be used for a quilted, winter pramsuit or an outdoor playsuit. Quilted fabric should have terylene wadding to ensure good washability. Hard-wearing denim-type fabrics, stretch towelling and stretch velour are all suitable for this garment, but check that your machine has a stretch stitch facility as stretch fabrics can be difficult to handle.

The body pattern is shown for ages 12 months to 2 years and for ages 3 – 4. The hood and sleeve patterns show all sizes.

Order of making

(See sewing techniques 2, 3, 14, 11 and 17.)

1 Stitch centre front seam from base of zip opening to bottom edge and insert zip.

2 Stitch centre back seam.

3 Stitch crutch seam and side seams.

4 Make hood.

5 Stitch hood to neckline.

6 Turn hems of sleeves and trousers, and insert elastic. Front edge of hood can be elasticated for a snug fit.

7 Make a matching belt.

To fit ages 1-2
RECTANGLE 60 x 72 cm

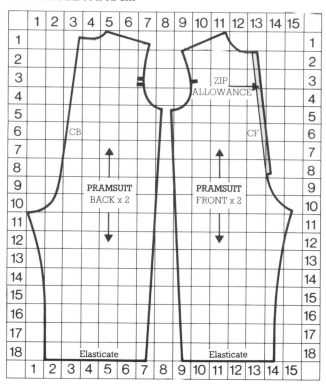

To fit ages 1-4
RECTANGLE 64 x 40 cm

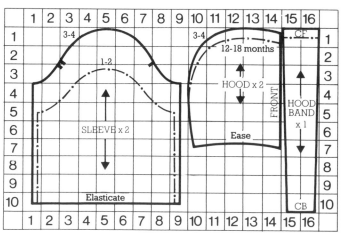

To fit ages 3-4
RECTANGLE 60 x 92 cm

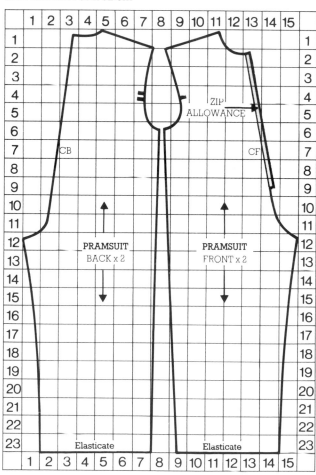

Painting Overall and Apron

Playing, painting, sticking or just 'helping' calls for a 'cover-up' of some type. This simple overall ties behind the neck and has a useful front pocket divided into three 'compartments'. Sleeves can be added from any pattern in the book and gathered at the wrists.

An apron pattern is given as an alternative and is ideal for cookery and barbecues.

PVC and shower curtaining are the obvious fabrics to use where water is concerned. To avoid pin-holes, use sticky tape to hold seams in position for stitching.

Painting overall

Order of making

(See sewing techniques 15, 1 and 2.)

1 Make pocket and bind top edge. Place on bottom front edge of apron and stitch two vertical strips of binding to create pocket compartments.

2 Stitch shoulder seams. Stitch side seams.

3 Bind round armholes and outside edge of overall, *except the neckline*.

4 Bind neckline, leaving long ends to tie behind neck.

Apron

Order of making

(This garment is cut without a side seam. See sewing techniques 15, 1 and 2.)

1 Make pocket and attach to centre front.

2 Bind across edge C-D and around sides and bottom edge A-B.

3 Bind sides A-C and D-B leaving long ends to tie behind neck and waist.

Alternative Simply hem all round apron, leaving a seam opening from A-C and D-B, through which you can thread a continuous cord.

To fit ages 2(3-4)5
RECTANGLE 36 x 40 cm

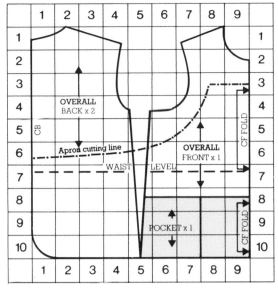

To fit ages 4(5-6-7)8
RECTANGLE 40 x 48 cm

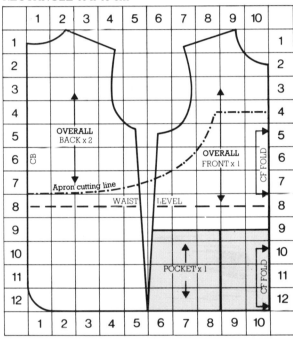

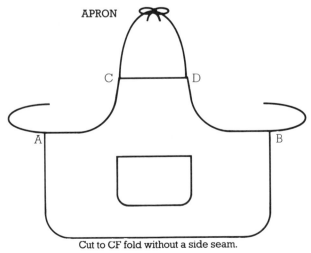

APRON

Cut to CF fold without a side seam.

Playsuit and Pinafore Dress

The bodice is the same on both these garments. Only the lower half changes. For best results use a soft fabric that will gather well: cotton, gingham, broderie anglais and voile are ideal. Both garments are made 'oversize' so they can be worn over jumpers and blouses. The sides are buttoned and the straps are stitched to the back and buttoned to the front. The bodice and the pockets should be fully lined. (The shaded area on the diagram indicates the original pattern from the basic bodice block on page 14.)

Bodice

Order of making

(See sewing techniques 17, 23 and 15.)

1 Make straps and stitch to back bodice.

2 Lay bodice front and back on lining, stitch round edges leaving waist open, and turn out.

3 Make pocket and stitch into position.

Trousers

Order of making

(See sewing techniques 2, 21, 18 and 11.)

1 Stitch side seams up to point X on diagram.

2 Stitch inside leg seams.

3 Stitch crutch seams.

4 Gather waist to fit bodice.

5 Stitch trousers to bodice. Add button and buttonhole fastening.

6 Turn up leg hems and elasticate.

Skirt

Order of making

(See sewing techniques 2, 21, 18 and 6.)

1 Stitch centre front and centre back seams.

2 Stitch side seams up to point X on diagram.

3 Gather waist to fit bodice.

4 Stitch skirt to bodice. Add button and buttonhole fastening.

5 Turn and stitch hem.

RECTANGLE 60 x 68 cm

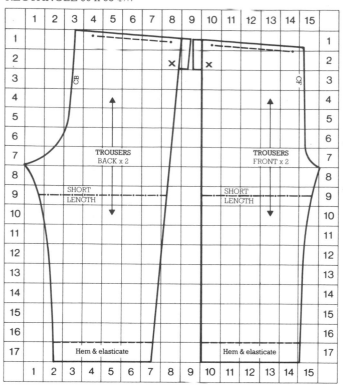

RECTANGLE 48 x 68 cm

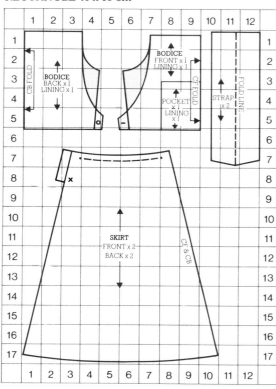

Suntop and Sarong

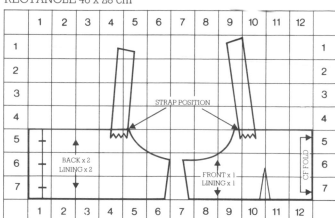

A touch of South Seas island magic! The suntop is lightly shaped with darts and fully lined. It buttons down the centre back. The sarong is a wrapover skirt that fastens with two buttons in the waistband. The diagram for this is on page 84. Recommended fabrics include any woven cotton or polyester cotton.

Order of making

(See sewing techniques 5, 17, 2, 23 and 18.)

Note The lining (which can be the main fabric) is made exactly as the main garment.

1 Stitch darts. Stitch side seams.

2 Make and attach straps to main fabric.

3 Making sure that straps are tucked inside, place lining and main fabric right sides together.

4 Stitch all round edges, leaving an opening through which the top can be turned to the right side. Turn the top to the right side. Close opening by hand sewing.

5 Make buttonholes and attach buttons to centre back.

To fit ages 4(5-6-7)8
RECTANGLE 40 x 28 cm

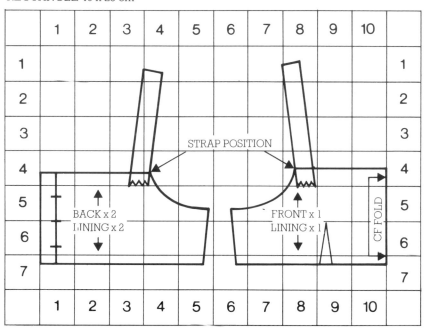

To fit ages 2(3-4)5
RECTANGLE 40 x 24 cm

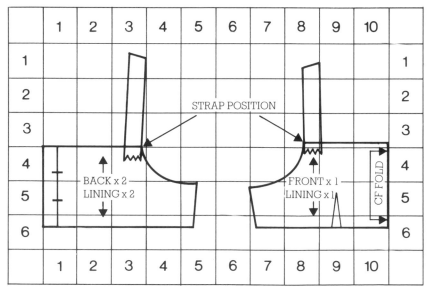

Jogging Top and Shorts

Made in stretch velour or towelling, this is an ideal outfit for a boy or girl. The top is made with raglan sleeves and a centre front zip to allow for easy fit. It has a pouch pocket across the front and all edges are bound with contrast binding. The back and sleeve diagrams are taken from the jacket pattern on page 60. The sleeve hems are elasticated, and a cord is threaded through the bottom hem to the centre front seam and tied to fit. This garment can be made into an anorak by omitting the pocket and inserting an open-ended zip.

The shorts are from the trousers diagram on page 50. They have an elasticated waist and are very easy to fit. Recommended fabrics include jersey, stretch towelling and velour.

Order of making

(See sewing techniques 14, 15, 1, 3, 11 and 6.)

1 Make hood and prepare pocket.

2 Bind front edge of hood, top of pocket and curved sides of pocket.

3 Stitch centre front seam, leaving an opening for zip. **Note** zip should be same colour as binding. Insert zip.

4 Position pocket and stitch it to front of top.

5 Stitch front sleeves to front of top. Stitch back sleeves to back of top.

6 Stitch hood to neckline.

7 Stitch side seams and sleeve seams in one operation.

8 Turn sleeve hems and insert elastic.

9 Turn hem of garment and insert either cord or elastic to size required.

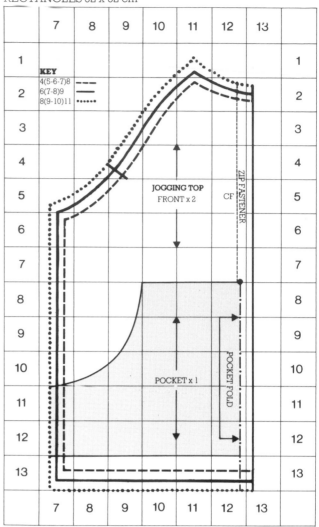

RECTANGLES 52 x 52 cm

KEY
4(5-6-7)8 -----
6(7-8)9 ———
8(9-10)11 ·······

JOGGING TOP
FRONT x 2

CF

ZIP FASTENER

POCKET x 1

POCKET FOLD

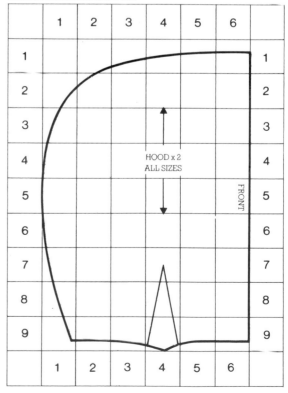

RECTANGLE 24 x 36 cm

HOOD x 2
ALL SIZES

FRONT

Bikini

The pattern is shown for three size ranges and can be combined with one of the elasticated skirts or beach tops to form a complete outfit. The bikini is fully lined and a good fit is ensured because it is cut on the cross grain of the fabric. The photograph shows rouleau ties made from the same fabric, but cord is equally suitable.

To fit ages 8(9-10)11
(up to hip 74 cm)
RECTANGLE 20 x 60 cm

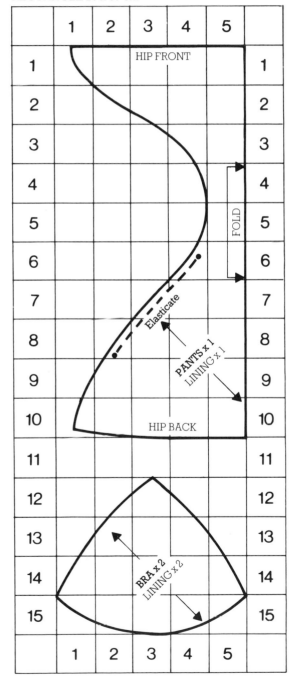

Bra top
Order of making

(See sewing techniques 17 and 2.)

1 Stitch a length of rouleau or cord to top point of main fabric, making sure it is long enough to tie behind neck.

2 Place lining and main fabric right sides together, *and with straps tucked inside*, stitch round outside edges, leaving about 1 cm unstitched at bottom corners to allow rouleau or cord to be threaded through.
Note An opening must be left for bra cups to be turned to right side after stitching.

3 Thread rouleau or cord through bottom of each bra cup, gathering and positioning bra as required. The back of the bra can either tie or be fastened with a special bra clip. Once in a satisfactory position, stitch the bra cup edges to keep them in place.

Pants
Order of making

(See sewing techniques 2 and 1.)

1 Place main fabric and lining right sides together and stitch round curved side seams, leaving hip back and front unstitched. Turn to right side.

2 Using long strips of bias binding, bind across hip back and front, leaving long ends to tie into bows at sides.

3 Stitch narrow elastic about 1 cm from edge of back leg hole (see diagram) to give a closer fit when worn.

To fit ages 4(5-6-7)8
(up to hip 66 cm)
RECTANGLE 16 x 56 cm

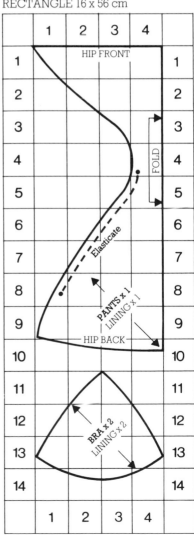

To fit ages 2(3-4)5
(up to hip 57 cm)
RECTANGLE 16 x 48 cm

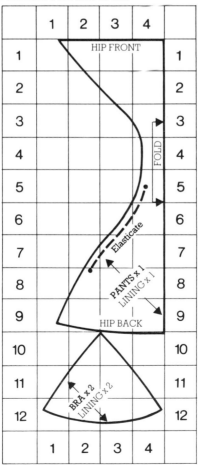

45

Beach Robe

This very simple T-shaped garment easily doubles as a dressing-gown for both boys and girls. You need only know the sleeve length and centre back length required to adapt the pattern to any size. The T-shape involves very little sewing, but if you want a more economical use of fabric, you can choose from the three other sleeve variations on the diagram.

To add detail, the pockets can be cut on the cross. Contrast binding finishes all the edges and can be used for a tie belt. Non-stretch towelling is ideal for the beach robe. The dressing-gown can be made in velour, wool tartan or brushed acrylic fabric.

Order of making

(See sewing techniques 15, 2, 1 and 17.)

1 Make and bind pockets, and stitch into position on front of garment.

2 Stitch shoulder seams.

3 Stitch side seams and sleeve seams in one operation.

4 Starting at a bottom side seam, bind all round outer edge of garment.

5 Make a rouleau or straight tie belt from fabric to match binding.

To fit ages 4(5-6-7)8
RECTANGLE 120 x 80 cm

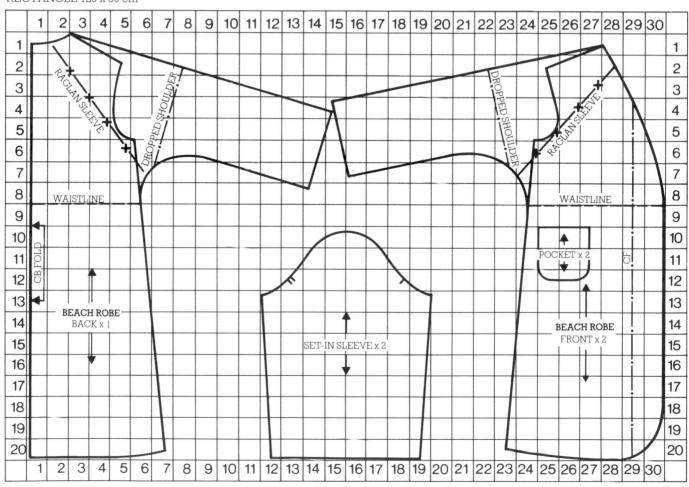

Sailor Dress

The low-waisted style of this dress is flattering and comfortable for all shapes and sizes. The neckline and armholes are bound, and a centre back zip closes the dress. The amount of gather in the skirt depends very much upon the type of fabric used; the finer the fabric, the more you can gather. Pleats can replace the gathers if you prefer. Recommended fabrics include any woven or jersey fabric. The sailor collar should be made from cotton piqué.

Order of making

(See sewing techniques 13, 2, 1, 3 or 18, 21 and 6.)

1 Make collar.

2 Stitch shoulder seams of bodice.

3 Stitch collar to neckline and bind neck edge.

4 Stitch side seams.

5 Bind armholes.

6 Check zip length required, measuring 2 cm up from bottom edge of bodice. Insert zip.

Note The zip can be replaced with centre back buttoning. Before cutting out, read the pattern and sewing instructions for the sun dress on page 71.

7 Stitch side seams and centre back seam of skirt.
Note The skirt can be cut without a centre back seam.

8 Gather skirt to fit bodice, and stitch together.

9 Turn and stitch hem.

RECTANGLE 20 x 32 cm

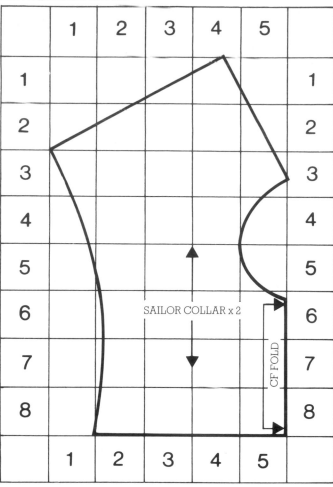

SAILOR COLLAR x 2

CF FOLD

To fit ages 8(9-10)11
RECTANGLE 48 x 48 cm   (Sizes 5–7 are on page 86)

ZIP ALLOWANCE

BODICE
BACK x 2

WAISTLINE

BODICE
FRONT x 1

CF FOLD

WAISTLINE

RECTANGLE 90 x 52 cm

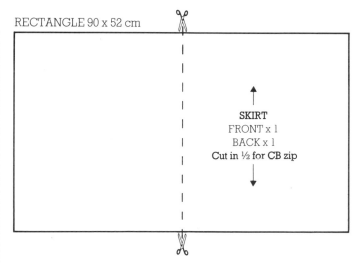

SKIRT
FRONT x 1
BACK x 1
Cut in ½ for CB zip

48

Trousers and Shirt

This simple trouser pattern is diagrammed for three lengths: shorts, pedal pushers and long trousers. All have elasticated waists. Pockets can be added in any position, if required, and the legs can be widened or narrowed at the side seams as fashion demands. Although the pattern shows shaped side seams, you can easily cut each leg as one piece *without the side seam*. Recommended fabrics include needlecord, corduroy, denim, worsted, Trevira and flannel. If made in cotton velvet, these trousers are ideal for a page boy outfit. Remember to cut the velvet in one direction only to avoid 'shading'.

The shirt is made to a traditional pattern with front and back yoke, long cuffed sleeves and centre front buttons and buttonholes. The diagram for this garment is on page 74.

Order of making

(See sewing techniques 2, 11 and 6.)

Note Each leg is made up separately.

1 Stitch side seams of each leg.

2 Stitch inside leg seams of each leg. (If you want front and back creases make them now.

Fold each leg with inside seam 2 cm to front of side seams and press.)

3 Stitch crutch seam.

4 Turn and stitch top hem casing, leaving a centre back opening through which to thread elastic.

5 Turn and stitch hems of each leg.

To fit ages 4(5-6-7)8
RECTANGLE 56 x 84 cm

To fit up to:

CRUTCH	52 cm
WAIST (FULLY STRETCHED)	69 cm
INSIDE LEG	51 cm

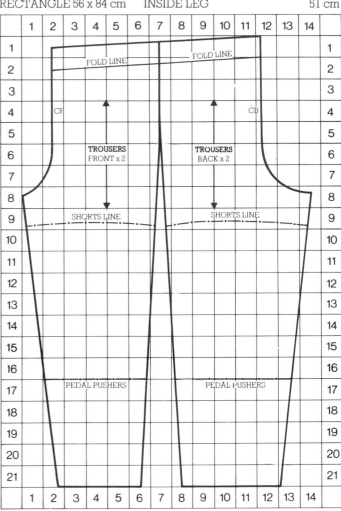

To fit ages 2(3-4)5
RECTANGLE 48 x 72 cm

To fit up to:

CRUTCH	45 cm
WAIST (FULLY STRETCHED)	60 cm
INSIDE LEG	43 cm

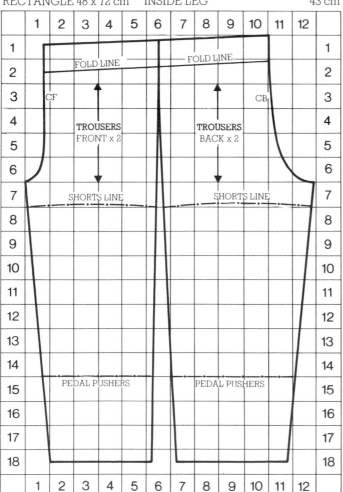

Tiered Skirt and Bolero Blouse

Here is a summery outfit that every girl will want to wear. The skirt can be made to any length and waist size, and minimal sewing is required. The tiers make it possible to use remnants of fabric, perhaps creating a mix-and-match effect. In our photograph the tier is emphasized by the use of a border print fabric. The skirt has a centre back seam and an elasticated waist. Pleats may be used instead of gathers in the lower tier. Follow steps a, b and c to make the pattern.

The 'cropped' blouse buttons down the back. It can be made sleeveless with bound armholes, or have set-in sleeves, again emphasized with the bordered fabric. Recommended fabrics include polyester cotton, lawn and soft denim, all of which gather easily. The pattern diagrams for the blouse are on page 97.

a Cut a rectangle to the size you require based on the instructions below.

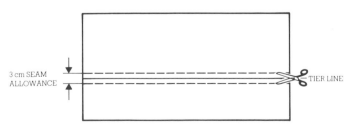

b Decide the level at which you want to make tiers and draw a straight line across your pattern.

c To give sufficient gather, the lower tier must be at least 1½ times wider than the top tier. (Twice as wide would be ideal.)

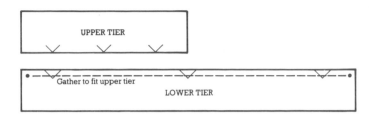

Order of making
(See sewing techniques 2, 11 and 6.)

1 Stitch seam to make each tier into a tube.

2 Gather bottom tier to fit top tier or pleat to fit (see note below) and stitch together.

3 Turn top hem and insert elastic.

4 Turn and stitch bottom hem.

Note If you prefer, the lower tier can be made with knife pleats or inverted pleats. Both require the tier to measure three times the circumference of the top tier.

Knife pleats

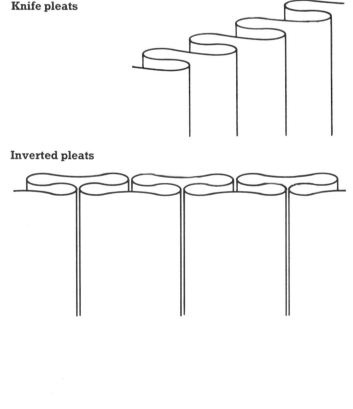

Inverted pleats

Tracksuit

Tracksuit, jogging suit, pyjamas? This pattern has many uses and can be made to look very different, for each type of use. It must be made in stretch fabric, velour or jersey being ideal, and you can use contrast trim for binding, cuffs and inserts. Your machine should have a stretch stitch facility for successful seaming. Special needles are available. Velour fabric (like velvet) must be cut with the pile running in one direction only.

Note If you are using contrast *insert bands:*

a Mark the position carefully on the basic pattern.

b Write TOP on each piece *before* cutting the bands.

c Cut the bands out of the pattern (the shaded areas) and remember that each cut edge must have a seam allowance added.

To change the size of this pattern see the pattern grading section on pages 12 – 17.

Top

Order of making
(See sewing techniques 22, 7, 1, 2 and 9.)

1 Stitch contrast bands into front bodice.

2 Stitch front sleeves to front. Stitch back sleeves to back.

3 Bind neckline.

4 Stitch side seams and sleeve seams in one operation.

5 Make wrist bands and bodice band.

6 Lightly gather bottom of sleeves and bottom of bodice. Attach wrist bands and bodice band.

Trousers

Order of making
(See sewing techniques 2, 11 and 9.)

Note Trouser legs are made separately. Contrast bands should be stitched in place before making up begins.

1 Stitch side seams.

2 Stitch inside leg seams.

3 Stitch crutch seams.

4 Turn and stitch top hem and insert elastic.

5 Make ankle bands.

6 Lightly gather legs and attach bands.

RECTANGLE 36 x 56 cm

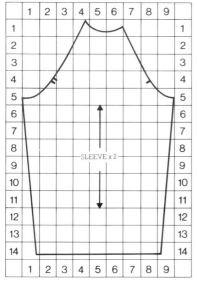

To fit ages 8(9-10)11

CHEST	76–82 cm
CB LENGTH	32 cm
CRUTCH	52–53 cm
INSIDE LEG	54 cm
WAIST (STRETCHED)	68–76 cm

RECTANGLE 62 x 14 cm

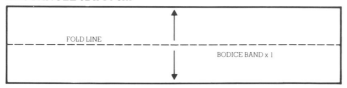
FOLD LINE
BODICE BAND x 1

RECTANGLE 32 x 14 cm

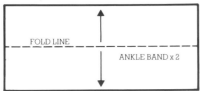
FOLD LINE
ANKLE BAND x 2

RECTANGLE 20 x 12 cm

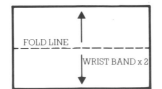
FOLD LINE
WRIST BAND x 2

RECTANGLE 52 x 84 cm

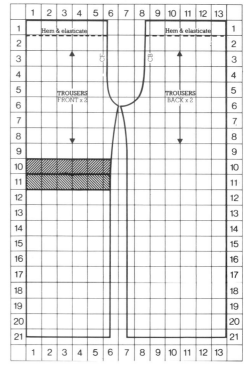
Hem & elasticate   Hem & elasticate
TROUSERS FRONT x 2   TROUSERS BACK x 2

RECTANGLE 48 × 36 cm

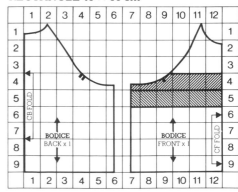
BODICE BACK x 1   BODICE FRONT x 1

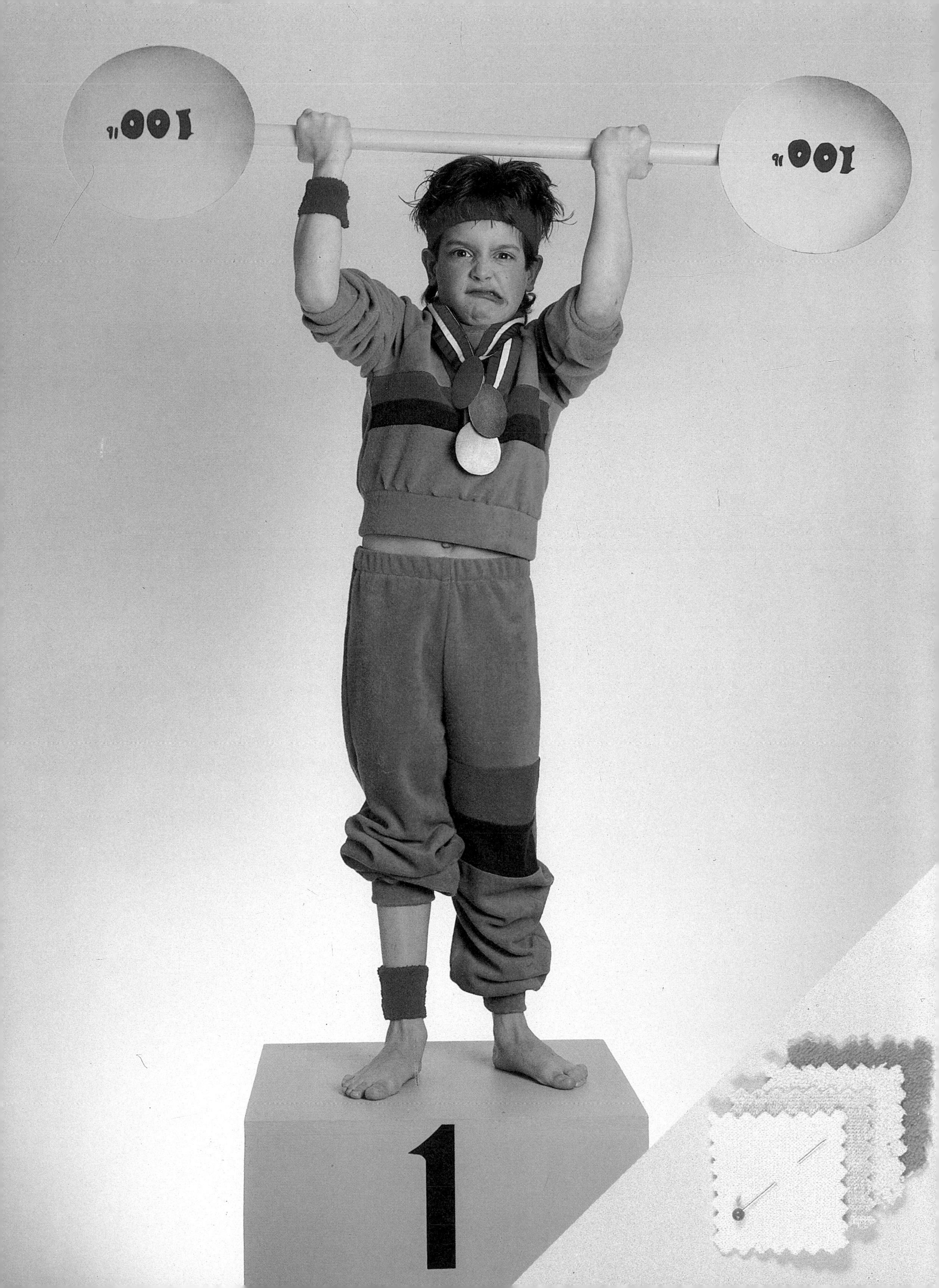
1

Pretty Print Dress

This classic dress with a raised waistline is easily adapted to a full-length bridesmaid dress. The neckline is trimmed with ready-frilled broderie anglais and bound with the main fabric. The puffed sleeves are gathered into a small cuff. The bodice is diagrammed with darts, but these can be omitted if you prefer. The dress is fastened with a centre back zip and a sash can be made to give a closer fit.

Suitable fabrics include silk, cotton or any fine woven fabric that does not require lining.

Order of making

(See sewing techniques 5, 2, 7, 8, 25, 1, 21, 3, 6 and 17.)

1 Stitch all darts.

2 Stitch shoulder seams.

3 Gather sleeve heads to fit armholes.

4 Gather bottom of sleeves to fit cuffs.

5 Stitch sleeves into armholes.

6 Stitch side seams and sleeve seams in one operation.

7 Make cuffs.

8 Stitch cuffs to sleeves.

9 Attach frilling to neckline, then bind neck.

10 Stitch side seams of skirt, and centre back seam from base of zip opening to bottom edge.

11 Gather skirt to fit bodice and stitch together.

12 Insert zip.

13 Turn and stitch hem.

14 Make a contrast or matching sash.

RECTANGLE 36 x 24 cm

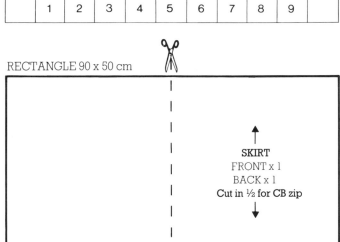
SLEEVE x 2

RECTANGLE 90 x 50 cm

SKIRT
FRONT x 1
BACK x 1
Cut in ½ for CB zip

RECTANGLE 26 x 10 cm

FOLD LINE
CUFF x 2

To fit ages 4(5-6-7)8
(Sizes 8–11 are on page 58)
RECTANGLE 40 x 32 cm

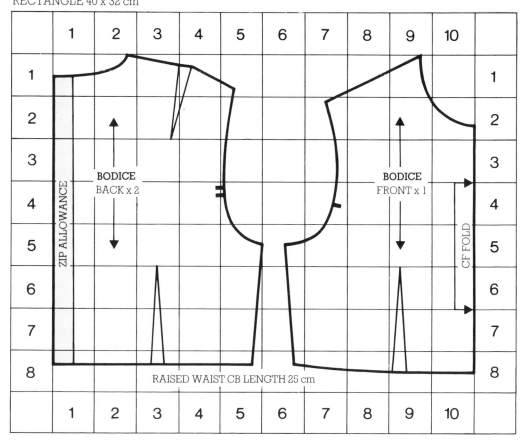

ZIP ALLOWANCE

BODICE
BACK x 2

BODICE
FRONT x 1

CF FOLD

RAISED WAIST CB LENGTH 25 cm

Party Dress

This very pretty dress with a raised waist and cape sleeves is made in broderie anglais and fully lined. The lining can be made in a contrast colour for extra emphasis. The bodice is mounted on to the lining while the skirt lining is cut loose. The collar and sleeves are edged with guipure lace, and the sash is made in satin.

Although ideal for parties and special occasions, this pattern is also suitable for a confirmation dress.

RECTANGLE 48 x 28 cm

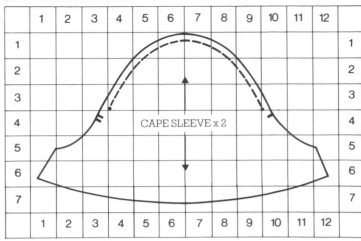

RECTANGLE 114 x 61 cm

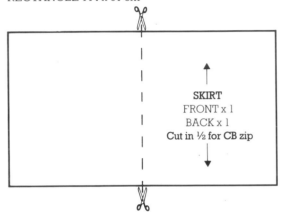

Order of making

(See sewing techniques 2, 5, 25, 1, 7, 6, 21, 3 and 17.)

1 Lay bodice on lining and stitch all round edges.

2 Stitch darts.
Note Darts can be elasticated or treated as gathers if you prefer.

3 Stitch shoulder seams.

4 Use purchased neck frilling or cut a strip of fabric 10 cm wide and twice neck size in length. Gather to fit neck edge.

5 Stitch frilling to neckline and bind neck edge.

6 Gather sleeve heads to fit armholes.

7 Stitch sleeves into armholes.

8 Stitch side seams and sleeve seams in one operation.

9 Hem sleeves.

10 Stitch side seams of skirt. Stitch centre back seam from base of zip opening to bottom edge.

11 Gather skirt to fit bodice and stitch together.

12 Insert zip.

13 Turn and stitch hem.

14 Make contrast or matching sash.

To fit ages 8(9-10)11   (Sizes 4–8 are on page 56)
RECTANGLE 44 x 40 cm

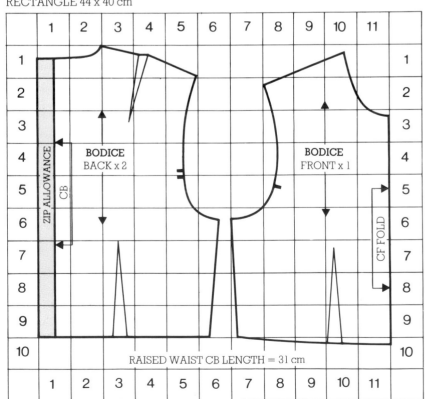

Jacket

Fully lined in colourful brushed cotton, this needlecord jacket will be popular with all ages. The three size ranges shown will make up with more ease than other garments in the book and the raglan sleeves give room for thick sweaters underneath for extra warmth. The wide wrapover front is closed with poppers and there are large patch pockets on the sides. The bottom of the jacket is simply hemmed, but you can add a cord fastening or elastication if you prefer.

As there is a lot of room for movement and extra layers underneath, please check and understand your pattern for fit before cutting out your fabric. Recommended fabrics include needlecord, corduroy and gaberdine.

RECTANGLE 44 x 44 cm

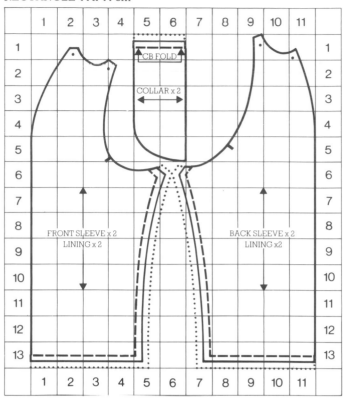

Order of making

(See sewing techniques 15, 7, 13, 2, 11 and 18 or 16.)

1 Make and attach side pockets to fronts of jacket pieces.

2 Stitch front sleeves to front armholes.
Stitch back sleeves to back armholes.

3 Stitch top sleeve seams.

4 Make collar and stitch to neckline of *main fabric,* carefully matching centre back neck.

5 Stitch side seams and sleeve seams in one operation.

6 Make the lining by following steps 2, 3 and 5.

7 Turn lining inside out and push sleeves of main garment into sleeves of lining. You should now have two *right* sides facing each other.

8 Starting at bottom edge of centre back, stitch right round outer edges, leaving sufficient opening at back to turn

garment through to right side. (This opening will be closed by hand sewing.) Turn garment to right side, pushing lining sleeves down main fabric armholes as you do so.

9 Turn and stitch sleeve hems, inserting elastic if required.

10 Make buttons and buttonholes or use popper fastenings down centre front.

To fit ages 4-11
RECTANGLE 52 x 52 cm

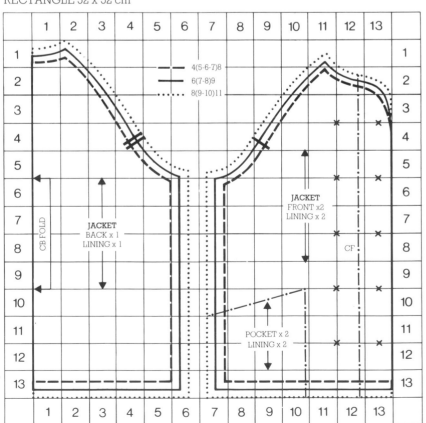

Waisted Dress

This is a classic dress pattern often used for school dresses, but highly fashionable in any modern fabric. It has a round collar, front button opening and long cuffed sleeves. The diagram includes a separate front facing, which can be cut in contrast fabric, perhaps matching the cuffs and collar. The waistline can be elasticated *after* the skirt is attached if you want a closer fit, or you can make a tie belt from matching fabric. The pattern gives two sleeve variations — a short, puffed sleeve and a long sleeve with frilled wrist.

Recommended fabrics include brushed cotton, lawn and any woven fabric. Checks and stripes that require matching should be avoided.

Order of making

(See sewing techniques 2, 13, 4, 7, 8, 18, 21 and 6.)

1 Stitch shoulder seams.

2 Make and attach collar to neckline.

3 Stitch front facings to front edge and around front neckline, enclosing collar.

4 Gather sleeve heads to fit armholes.

5 Stitch side seams of bodice. Stitch sleeve seams.

6 Make cuffs and stitch small hem openings at bottom of sleeves.

7 Gather sleeves to fit cuffs and attach cuffs.

8 Stitch sleeves into armholes.

9 Make buttonholes and attach buttons.

10 Stitch side seams of skirt, and gather skirt evenly to fit bodice.

11 Stitch skirt to bodice.

12 Turn and stitch hem.

To fit ages 4(5-6-7)8 (Sizes 8–11 are on page 102)
RECTANGLE 40 x 52 cm

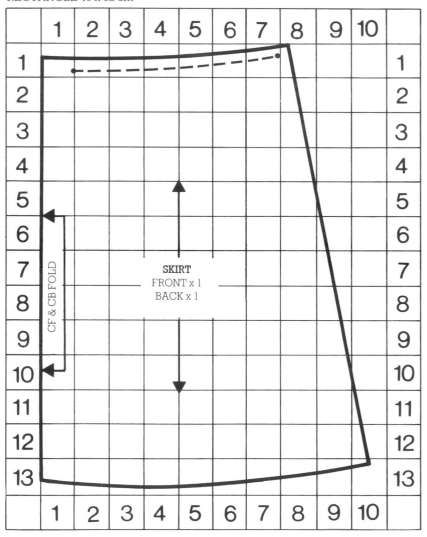

RECTANGLE 32 x 52 cm

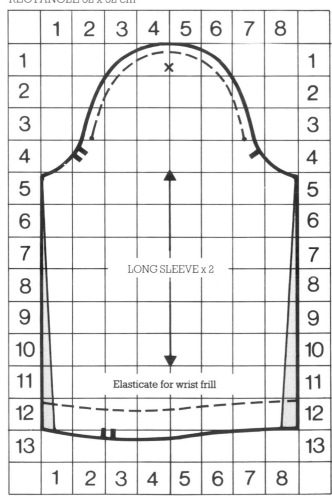

RECTANGLE 44 x 36 cm

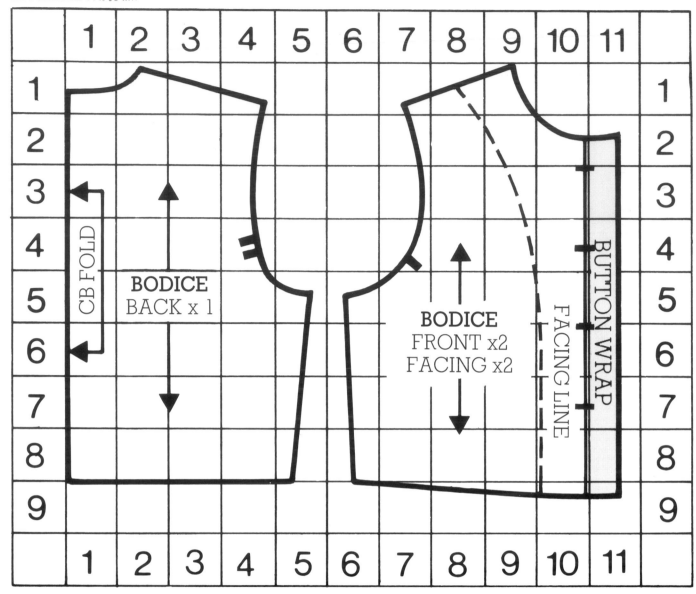

| | 1 | 2 | 3 | 4 | 5 | 6 | 7 | 8 | 9 | 10 | 11 | |

BODICE BACK x 1

CB FOLD

BODICE FRONT x2 FACING x2

FACING LINE

BUTTON WRAP

RECTANGLE 40 x 24 cm

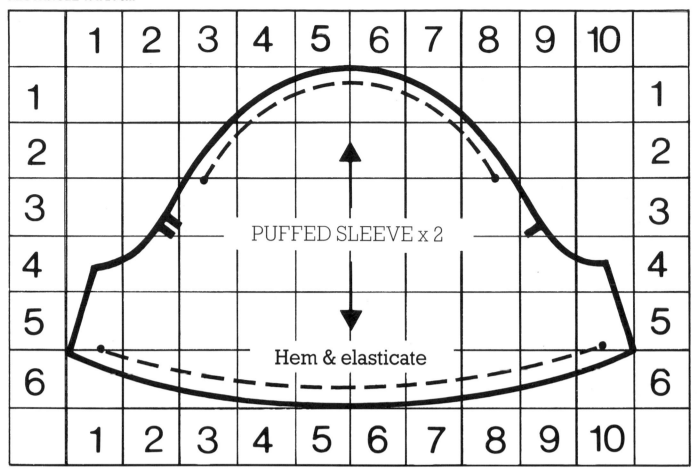

	1	2	3	4	5	6	7	8	9	10	
1											1
2											2
3				PUFFED SLEEVE x 2							3
4											4
5						Hem & elasticate					5
6											6
	1	2	3	4	5	6	7	8	9	10	

RECTANGLE 16 x 20 cm

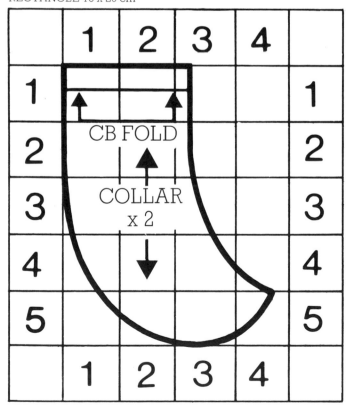

	1	2	3	4	
1					1
2	CB FOLD				2
3	COLLAR x 2				3
4					4
5					5
	1	2	3	4	

RECTANGLE 20 x 8 cm

	1	2	3	4	5	
1		CUFF x 2				1
2						2
	1	2	3	4	5	

School Blouse and Skirt

This simple blouse buttons down the front and is ideal as school wear for both boys and girls. It can also be made without the top button and buttonhole to give an open-necked collar with revers. There are two sleeve and collar variations. From the diagram you can see that it is an easy pattern to take to any length. Suitable fabrics include cotton, polyester cotton and Viyella.

The school skirt has an inverted front pleat, in-seam pockets and a centre back zip. Accurate hip measurements are *vital* for a good, smooth fit.

The universal skirt pattern shows how to make the school skirt to *any size* and how to adapt it to a simple flared shape. Suitable fabrics include Trevira, worsted and flannel. Tartan or check fabrics need careful matching at the side seams, so ensure that you buy enough.

Skirt

Order of making

(See sewing techniques 10, 2, 3, 15, 18 and 6.)

Note Waistband patterns are not given on the diagrams. See sewing technique 10. The waistband should be made *before* starting the skirt.

1 Make waistband.

2 Stitch centre back seam from base of zip opening to bottom edge of skirt. Insert zip.

3 Stitch inverted front pleat from waistband to required depth.

4 Attach pockets to side seams. Stitch side seams.

5 Attach waistband, adding button and buttonhole or hook and bar fastening.

6 Turn and stitch hem.

Blouse

Order of making

(See sewing techniques 13, 8, 2, 15, 7, 6 and 18.)

1 Make collar.

2 Make cuffs.

3 Stitch shoulder seams.

4 Make and attach pocket.

5 Stitch collar to neckline, using front fold line to enclose raw edges.

6 Gather sleeve heads to fit armholes and stitch into place.

7 Stitch side seams and sleeve seams of bodice in one operation.

8 Cuffed sleeve: Make small hem opening at bottom of sleeves. Pleat or gather sleeve bottom to fit cuffs. Attach cuffs.
 Frilled sleeve: Stitch a small hem at bottom of sleeves and then elasticate in position indicated.

9 Machine hem bodice.

10 Make buttonholes and attach buttons.

To fit ages 4(5-6-7)8

RECTANGLE 36 x 48 cm

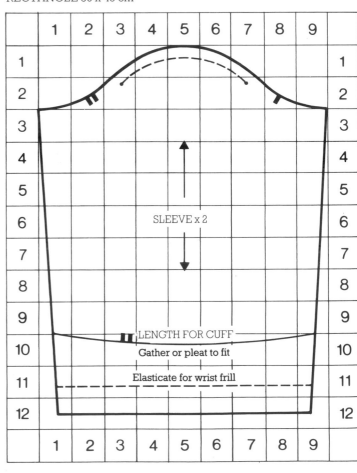

SLEEVE x 2

LENGTH FOR CUFF
Gather or pleat to fit
Elasticate for wrist frill

RECTANGLE 56 x 48 cm

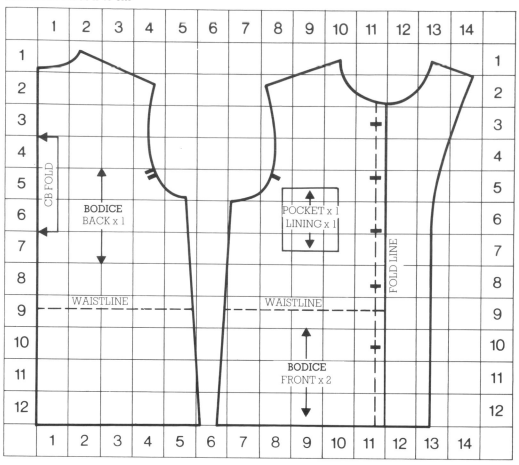

	1	2	3	4	5	6	7	8	9	10	11	12	13	14	
1															1
2															2
3															3
4															4
5															5
6															6
7															7
8															8
9															9
10															10
11															11
12															12
	1	2	3	4	5	6	7	8	9	10	11	12	13	14	

CB FOLD

BODICE
BACK x 1

POCKET x 1
LINING x 1

FOLD LINE

WAISTLINE   WAISTLINE

BODICE
FRONT x 2

RECTANGLE 20 x 20 cm

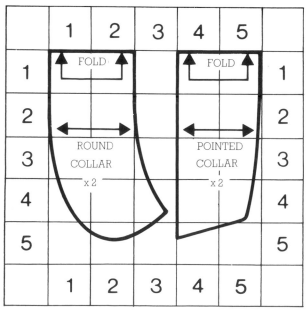

	1	2	3	4	5	
1	FOLD			FOLD		1
2						2
3	ROUND COLLAR x 2			POINTED COLLAR x 2		3
4						4
5						5
	1	2	3	4	5	

RECTANGLE 24 x 16 cm

	1	2	3	4	5	6	
1							1
2			FOLD LINE				2
3		CUFF x 2					3
4							4
	1	2	3	4	5	6	

Universal skirt pattern

Order of making

This is the easiest of patterns to draft to any size. Diagram 1 is a basic skirt pattern that can be converted to any style of skirt. Diagram 2 shows how to adapt it to a flared skirt and a skirt with an inverted front pleat.

1 Follow the diagram to create the basic skirt pattern.

2 Cut up dotted line to base of dart.

3 Fold out dart. This opens hem to form the flare.

4 Centre front and centre back can be cut to a fold allowing a side zip to be inserted.

5 An inverted pleat can be added to centre front.

6 A centre back seam can be added to avoid a side zip and allow the use of in-seam pockets.

To fit ages 4(5-6-7)8
RECTANGLE 36 x 52 cm

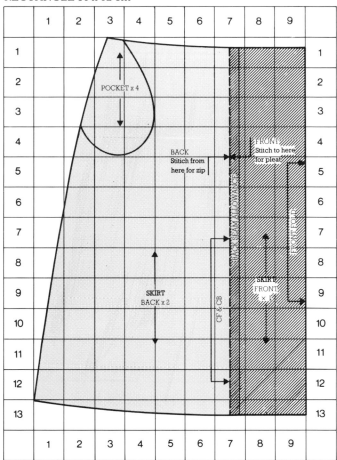

	1	2	3	4	5	6	7	8	9	
1										1
2			POCKET x 4							2
3										3
4										4
5						BACK Stitch from here for zip		FRONT Stitch to here for pleat		5
6										6
7										7
8										8
9				SKIRT BACK x 2			CF & CB	SKIRT FRONT x 1		9
10										10
11										11
12										12
13										13
	1	2	3	4	5	6	7	8	9	

BACK SEAM ALLOWANCE — FRONT FOLD

WAISTBAND TO SIZE (Sewing technique 10)

DIAGRAM 1

¼ WAIST + 3 cm

1 cm

1.5 cm DART

8 cm

Check hip fitting here

LENGTH + 5 cm HEM

CF & CB

¼ LARGEST HIP SIZE + 3 cm

DIAGRAM 2

POCKET x 4

CF & CB

FOLD OF FABRIC

Sundress

With narrow straps and a low-waisted bodice, this is the perfect dress for hot summer days. The garment buttons down the left-hand side and can be made in any woven fabric, but it is best to avoid large checked patterns.

Order of making

(See sewing techniques 17, 4, 2, 18, 21 and 6.)

1 Make straps.

2 Stitch straps to front and back bodice.

3 Stitch facings to top edge and to left-hand side of front and back bodice.

4 Stitch right-hand side seam including facing.

5 Make buttonholes and attach buttons to left side.

6 Stitch side seams and centre back seam of skirt.

7 Gather skirt to fit bodice and stitch together.

8 Turn and stitch hem.

To fit ages 4(5-6-7)8

RECTANGLE 44 x 32 cm

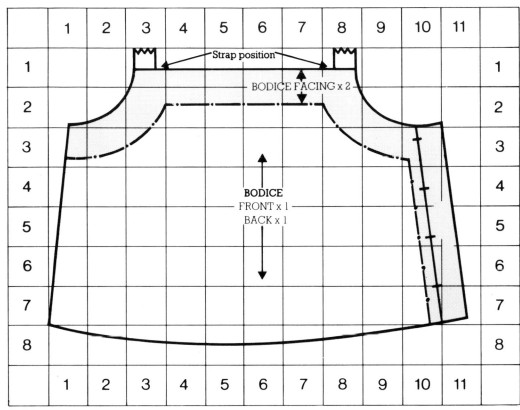

RECTANGLE 90 x 43 cm

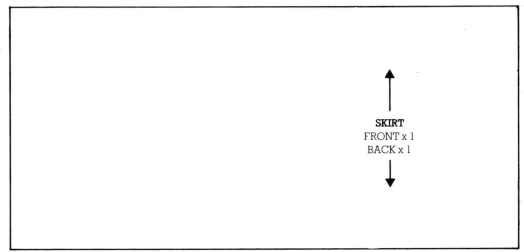

Pinafore Dress and Blouse

This neat pinafore dress is high-waisted and has a fully lined bodice and front pocket. It is fastened with a centre back zip. Recommended fabrics include needlecord, denim and firm jersey.

The Viyella blouse has a Peter Pan-type collar, long frilled sleeves and a front button fastening. Recommended fabrics include polyester cotton, brushed cotton and Viyella. The blouse diagrams and instructions are on page 66.

Order of making

(See sewing techniques 2, 15, 21, 3 and 6.)

1 Stitch shoulder seams of garment. Stitch shoulder seams of lining.

2 Stitch pocket to pocket lining, leaving bottom edge open. Turn to right side.

3 Stitch lining to bodice, leaving side seams open, and turn to right side.

4 Stitch pocket to centre front, matching bottom edges.

5 Stitch side seams of bodice and lining.

6 Stitch side seams of skirt. Stitch centre back seam from base of zip opening to bottom edge.

7 Gather skirt to fit bodice.

8 Stitch skirt to bodice, matching side seams and centre front.

9 Insert zip.

10 Turn and stitch hem.

SKIRTS

2 (3-4) 5	4 (5-6-7) 8	8 (9-10) 11
RECTANGLE 60 × 40 cm	RECTANGLE 80 × 51 cm	RECTANGLE 90 × 64 cm
All skirts are cut as two rectangles with one piece cut in half vertically for centre back zip.		

To fit ages 2(3-4)5
RECTANGLE 36 x 24 cm

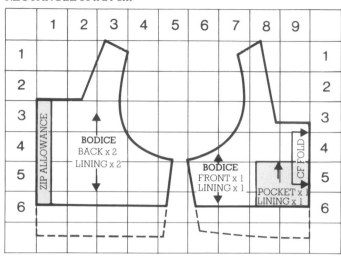

To fit ages 4(5-6-7)8
RECTANGLE 44 x 28 cm

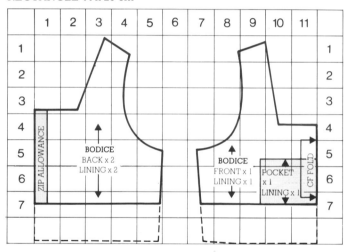

To fit ages 8(9-10)11
RECTANGLE 52 x 32 cm

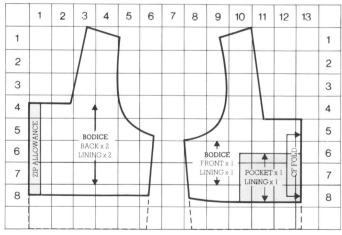

Safari Shirt and Shorts

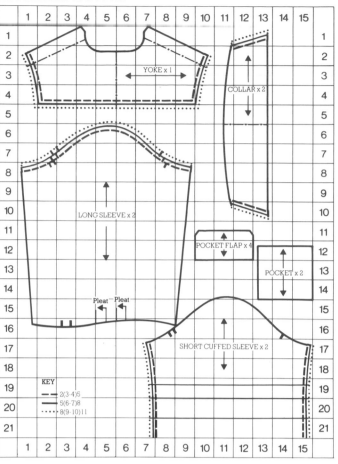

RECTANGLE 60 x 84 cm

This is a loose-fitting shirt with a front and back yoke-line, short cuffed sleeves and optional breast pockets. A diagram for long sleeves is also included. The small check fabric we used in the photograph allows easy matching at the centre front where the shirt is fastened with buttons or poppers. Recommended fabrics include cotton, lawn and polyester cotton. The grading lines on the diagrams show how the size is increased. As this shirt if usually worn slightly oversize, you should check with your control block which size you want to make. The shorts, which can be lined, are made from the trouser diagram on page 50.

Order of making

(See sewing techniques 26, 2, 13, 15, 7, 8, 6 and 18.)

1 Stitch back of shirt to back yoke.

2 Stitch fronts of shirt to front yokes.

3 Make collar and stitch to neckline.

4 Using fold line at centre front, enclose collar at top edge.

5 Make and attach pockets and pocket flaps.

6 Stitch sleeves into armholes.

7 Long sleeves: Turn small hem opening at bottom of sleeves.

8 Stitch side seams and sleeve seams in one operation.

9 Make cuffs. Pleat sleeve bottom to fit cuffs and attach cuffs to sleeves.

10 Short cuffed sleeve: Omit steps 7 and 9. Press, turn and hem cuffs.

11 Machinc hcm shirt.

12 Make buttonholes and attach buttons.

To fit ages 4-11
RECTANGLE 60 x 48 cm

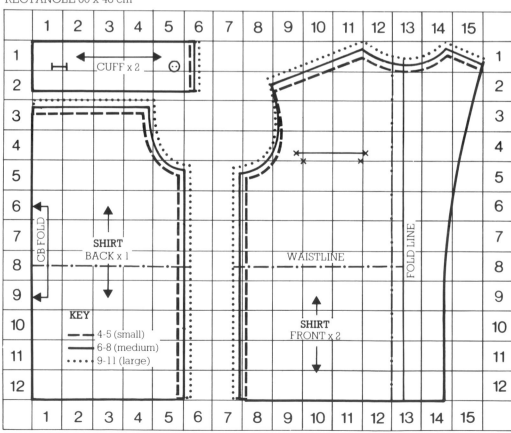

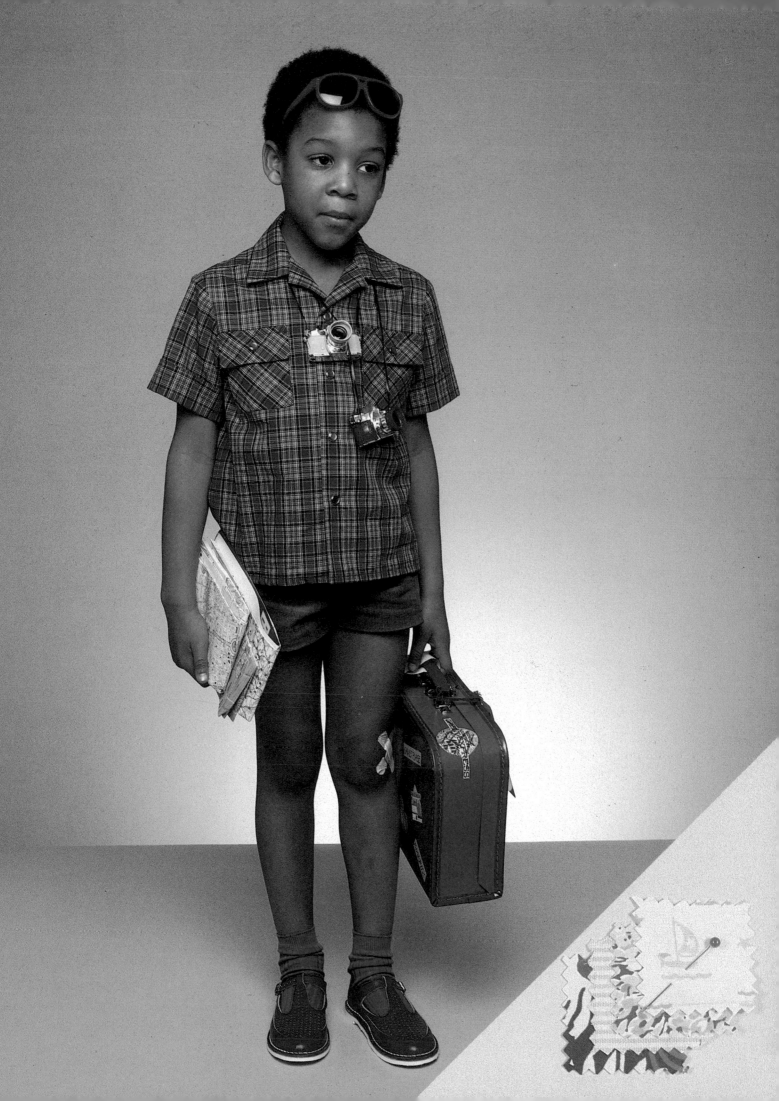

Sleeveless Nightdress

This loose-fitting nightdress with lined bodice and tie shoulders matches the quilted dressing-gown on page 78. It can be made to any length as the skirt is simply cut from two rectangles of 90 cm fabric. (Don't forget to add a hem!) Recommended fabrics include cotton, lawn and voile.

Order of making

(See sewing techniques 2, 21 and 6.)

1 Stitch bodice back and front to lining, leaving side seams and bottom edge open.

2 Stitch side seams of bodice and lining in one operation, and turn right side out.

3 Stitch side seams of skirt.

4 Gather skirt to fit bodice.

5 Stitch skirt to bodice.

6 Turn and stitch hem.

To fit ages 8(9-10)11
RECTANGLE 48 x 48 cm

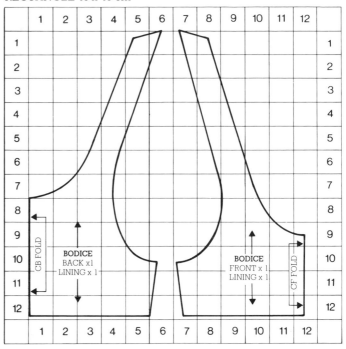

To fit ages 4(5-6-7)8
RECTANGLE 40 x 40 cm

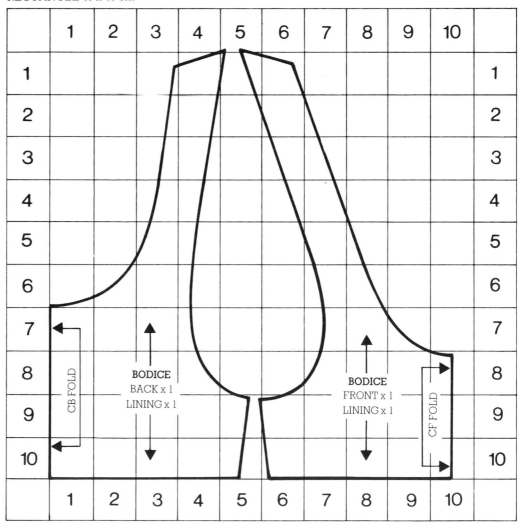

77

Quilted Dressing-gown

Made in warm quilted fabric for chilly nights, this dressing-gown matches the nightdress on page 77. It can be made with set-in, kimono or raglan sleeves, and has optional pockets. As buttonholes can be difficult to make on quilted fabric, it is suggested that you use poppers, or attach ribbon loops and buttons similar to the fastenings on a duffel coat.

The dressing-gown can be made in brushed acrylic fabric, tartan wool or quilted cotton.

Order of making

(See sewing techniques 15, 2, 13, 7, 16 and 6.)

1 Make pockets and stitch to fronts of garment.

2 Stitch shoulder seams.

3 Make collar. Stitch collar to neckline, folding back front edge and enclosing collar at top edge. Catchstitch facing at shoulder line.

4 Gather sleeve heads to fit armholes and stitch into place.

5 Stitch side seams and sleeve seams in one operation.

6 Hem sleeves.

7 Attach poppers, or loops and buttons to garment.

8 Turn and stitch hem.

To fit ages 4(5-6-7)8
RECTANGLE 132 x 104 cm

RAGLAN SLEEVE
KIMONO SLEEVE
KIMONO SLEEVE
RAGLAN SLEEVE
WAISTLINE
WAISTLINE
FOLD
COLLAR x 2
POCKET x 2
CB FOLD
FOLD LINE
DRESSING-GOWN BACK x 1
SET-IN SLEEVE x 2
DRESSING-GOWN FRONT x 2

Long-sleeved Nightdress

This pretty nightdress has a centre-buttoning round yoke with inset frilling edged with lace at the neck and shoulders. The yoke is lined and the skirt is gathered to fit at back and front. All the frills are optional and an alternative collar pattern is shown in the diagram.

The nightdress is best made in a soft, flame-proof fabric, such as winceyette, Viyella or polyester cotton.

The pattern can also be used for a very pretty bridesmaid dress. Suitable fabrics include broderie anglais, lawn, satin and crêpe.

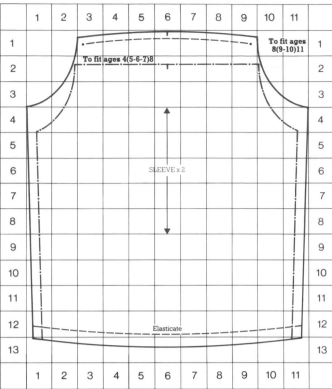

RECTANGLE 44 × 52 cm

Order of making

(See sewing techniques 13 or 25, 18, 2 and 6.)

1 Make collar or prepare frilled insert for neckline. You can purchase ready-made frilling or make your own from narrow fabric strips, which need to be *twice* as long as the neck size. Ribbon is very attractive when gathered or pleated into the neckline.

2 Stitch shoulder seams of yoke. Stitch shoulder seams of lining.

3 Stitch collar or frilling to neckline.

4 With collar or frilling inside, place lining yoke on outer yoke, right sides together, and stitch round neckline and down centre front edges.
   Turn section through to right side and stitch bottom circular edges together.

5 Make buttonholes in front yoke and stitch on buttons.

6 Stitch fronts of sleeves to front nightdress. Stitch backs of sleeves to back nightdress.

7 Matching centre back, centre front and centre shoulder seams, gather nightdress and sleeve heads to fit yoke.

8 Make sleeve frilling and stitch to yoke, using shoulder seam to centre frill position.

9 Stitch gathered nightdress and sleeve heads to yoke.

10 Stitch side seams and sleeve seams in one operation.

11 Insert elastic at wrists as required.

12 Turn and stitch hem.

To fit ages 4(5-6-7)8
RECTANGLE 52 x 80 cm

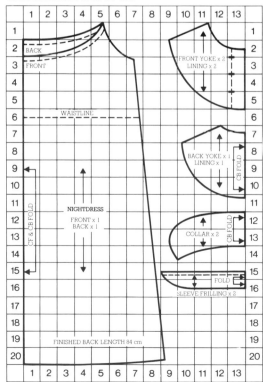

To fit ages 8(9-10)11
RECTANGLE 56 x 88 cm

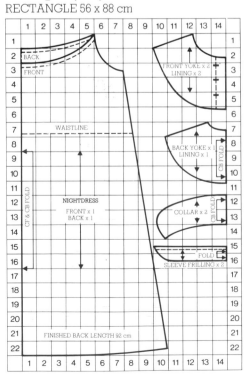

Unisex Pyjamas

This pattern is specially for use with stretch fabric, velour or jersey being most suitable.

The diagram pattern shows the top only, a simple T-shape, which can be adapted to a raglan or short sleeved version. The neck binding, and wrist and ankle bands look good in contrast fabric. You can also add a contrast band to the bottom of the bodice. If you choose not to, hem the bodice after step 2.

The trousers can be made from the tracksuit pattern (see page 54) or any other trouser pattern in the book.

Top

Order of making

(See sewing techniques 2, 1, 7 and 9.)

1 Stitch shoulder seams and bind neckline.

2 Stitch side seams and sleeve seams in one operation.

3 Make wrist, ankle and bodice bands.

4 Lightly gather bottom of bodice and sleeves.

5 Stitch bands to bodice.

To fit ages 3(4-5)6
RECTANGLE 44 x 40 cm

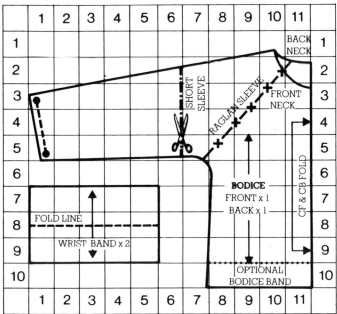

To fit ages 4(5-6-7)8
RECTANGLE 52 x 44 cm

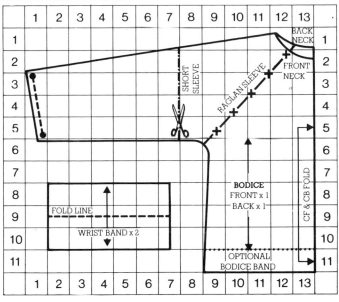

To fit ages 8(9-10)11
RECTANGLE 60 x 56 cm

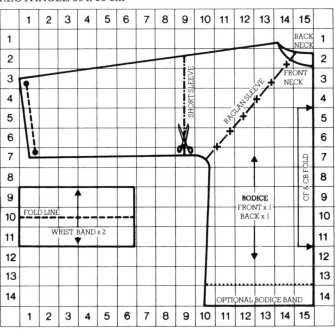

Wrapover Skirt

The unusual cut of this pattern allows the skirt to hang beautifully at the hem. Although the diagram shows only one size it can be easily altered to fit any size. Simply decrease or continue the centre back curve at waist and hem to the size required. To shorten or lengthen the pattern, adjust the centre-back and centre front length, and the curved line which forms the hem.

This garment can be made in a wide variety of fabrics, but is not suitable for checks or designs that need matching.

Order of making
(See sewing techniques 2, 20, 5, 10 and 6.)

Note The waistband is cut and made after the skirt has been tried on, and the exact size of band calculated.

1 Stitch centre back seam.

2 Wrapover skirt: Using a fusible interface webbing or neat stitching, secure fold on front edges.
   Sarong: This skirt requires only a small machined hem stitched continuously around the curved edges. Check length and stitch hem.

3 Matching centre fronts, try on skirt. Measure and cut waistband.

4 Make and attach waistband, adding buttonholes and buttons where required.

5 Wrapover skirt: Turn and stitch hem.

To fit waist 58-59 cm (finished length 46 cm)
RECTANGLE 80 x 60 cm

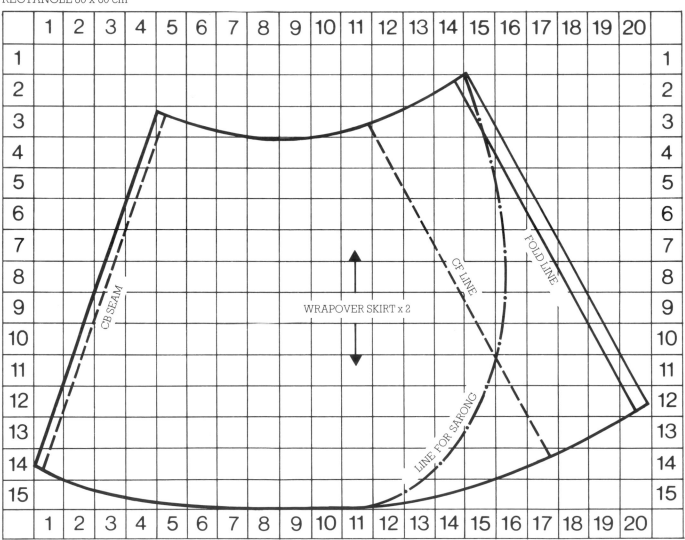

WRAPOVER SKIRT x 2
CB SEAM
CF LINE
FOLD LINE
LINE FOR SARONG

V-insert Dress

Mix-and-match jersey fabric makes this a very fashionable dress, and it can be made with or without the v-insert. The neckline is bound and a centre back zip fastens the dress. The sleeves are gathered into a wrist band, but a buttoned cuff is necessary if you make the dress in a woven fabric.

Order of making

(See sewing techniques 2, 7, 9, 21 and 6.)

1 Stitch v-insert into front bodice.

2 Stitch shoulder seams.

3 Bind neckline.

4 Gather sleeve heads to fit armholes.

5 Make wrist bands.

6 Gather bottom of sleeves to fit wrist bands.

7 Stitch side seams of bodice. Stitch sleeve seams.

8 Stitch wrist bands to sleeves and stitch sleeves into armholes.

9 Stitch side seams of skirt.

10 Gather skirt to fit bodice and stitch together.

11 Turn and stitch hem.

RECTANGLE 48 × 40 cm

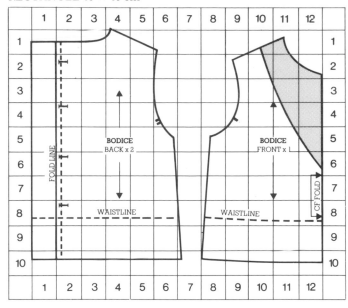

RECTANGLE 36 x 44 cm

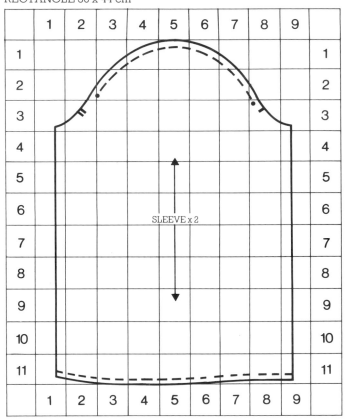

RECTANGLE 16 x 28 cm

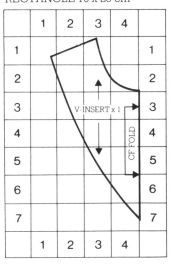

RECTANGLE 20 x 12 cm

RECTANGLE 90 x 43 cm

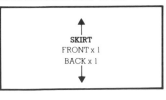

Duffel Coat

Children and adults alike find duffel coats comfortable and warm to wear. Our garment is a classic design with front and back yoke, hood, patch pockets and purchased toggle fastenings. The ideal fabric is a heavy coating with a contrast check on the reverse side. This does away with the need for a lining. Duffel coats tend to be worn shorter than other coats, so establish the finished length you require *before* you buy your fabric.

The shaded areas at the side seams on the pattern pieces allow you to cut the garment big enough to wear over several layers of clothes. For a lightweight summer coat, a closer fit can be obtained by using the inner cutting line. The yoke, which is fully lined, is additional to the garment and is stitched to the outside of the coat for warmth and decoration. For added interest it could be cut from suede, leather or contrast fabric.

A pattern is given for 'strap' fastenings which can be made from matching fabric. They are lined, have a buttonhole at either end and fasten to ordinary buttons sewn on the coat. Alternatively, strong popper fastenings may be used instead.

For the sleeves use the Basic Sleeve Block on page 16, increasing the width of the top arm fitting to match the sleeve head to the armhole of the duffel coat. The hood pattern is on page 42, but you can substitute the collar from page 60 if you prefer.

Order of making

(See sewing techniques 15, 19, 18, 14 or 13, 2, 7 and 6.)

Note Lap and fell seams are recommended for the main garment construction.

1 Make and prepare pockets.

2 Make strap fastenings, if using them, by placing fabric on lining, stitching round edges and leaving a small opening to turn straps through to right side. Press and close opening with hand sewing. Make buttonholes.

3 Stitch shoulders of yoke. Place right side down on lining and stitch all round outer edges, leaving neckline open.

Turn yoke to right side and press.

4 Make hood or prepare collar.

5 Stitch pockets to fronts of coat.

6 Stitch shoulder seams of coat.

7 Stitch hood or collar to *inside* of neckline.

8 Stitch yoke to neckline from inside of coat with lining side uppermost. Layer neckline seams.

9 Press yoke, which is now enclosing collar or hood to neckline, towards armhole edges and top stitch yoke to main garment.

10 Stitch sleeves into armholes.

11 Stitch side seams and sleeve seams in one operation.

12 Turn and stitch hem of coat and sleeve hems.

13 Attach front fastenings.

To fit ages 2(3-4)5
RECTANGLE 48 x 64 cm

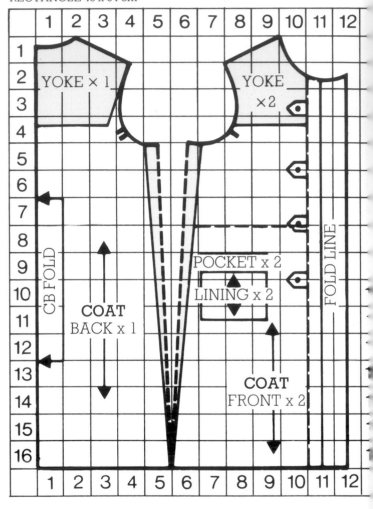

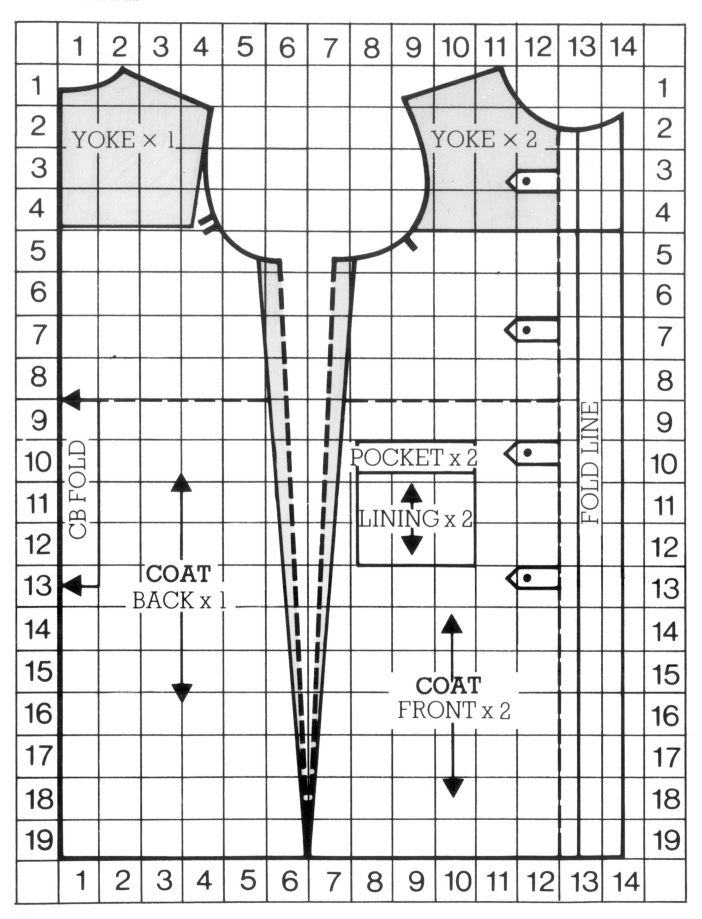

To fit ages 8(9-10)11
RECTANGLE 60 x 96 cm

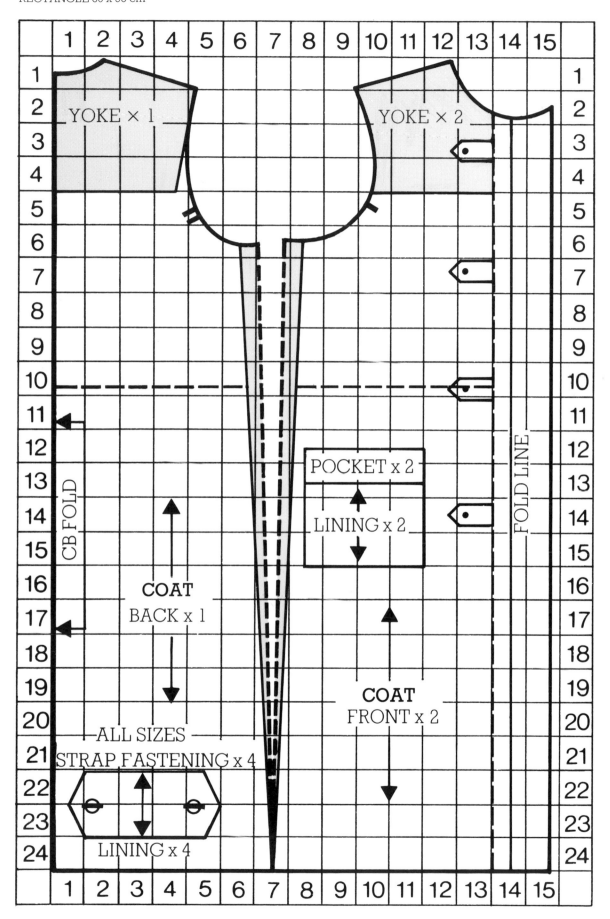

91

Velvet Dress

A special dress for special occasions is a must in every child's wardrobe. The ideal fabric is 100 per cent cotton velvet, which handles easily and looks good with very little pressing. Be sure to cut the fabric in one direction only to avoid 'shading'.

The neckline is trimmed with purchased frilling and bound. The sleeves, which can be long or short, are elasticated or frilled. A centre back zip fastens the garment. The contrast satin sash is cut on the cross to tie smoothly into a bow behind the waist. Recommended fabrics for the dress also include velveteen and non-stretch velour.

Order of making

(See sewing techniques 5, 2, 25, 7, 11, 21, 6 and 17.)

1 Stitch darts.

2 Stitch shoulder seams.

3 Stitch frilling to neckline and bind neck.

4 Gather sleeve heads to fit armholes.

5 Stitch side seams of bodice. Stitch sleeve seams.

6 Stitch sleeves into armholes.

7 Turn a small hem on sleeves and insert elastic to fit wrists comfortably.

8 Stitch side seams of skirt and centre back seam from base of zip opening to bottom edge of skirt.

9 Gather skirt to fit bodice and stitch together.

10 Turn and stitch hem.

11 Make a contrast or matching sash.

To fit ages 2(3-4)5 (Sizes 6–11 are on pages 56 and 58)

RECTANGLE 36 x 28 cm

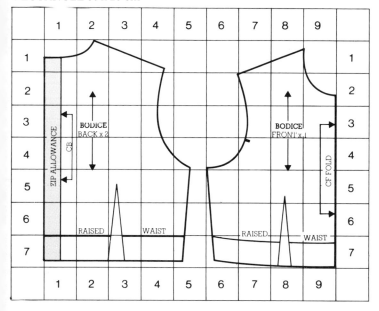

RECTANGLE 32 x 44 cm

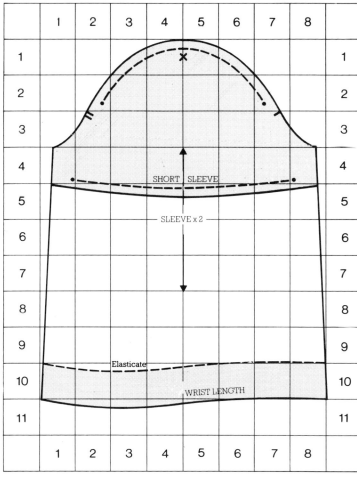

RECTANGLE 90 x 35 cm

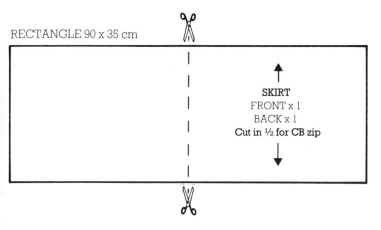

93

Victorian-style Pinafore

To fit ages 5-7
RECTANGLE 36 x 28 cm

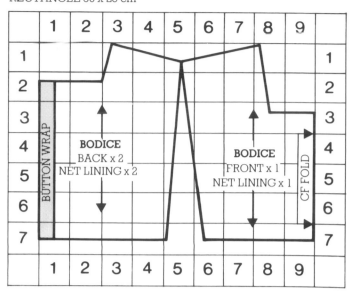

This high-waisted pinafore made in broderie anglais is a very attractive addition to any of the dresses. The bodice and pockets are lined with fine net to emphasize the pattern of the fabric. The pinafore buttons down the back of the bodice, leaving the skirt loose. Frilling emphasizes the position of the pockets. Recommended fabrics include broderie anglais and organza.

The dress pattern can be taken from the diagram on page 56 or 58, the only difference being that the sleeve is gathered near the bottom edge to form a frill. Recommended fabrics include cotton, lawn and pure silk.

RECTANGLE 40 x 56 cm

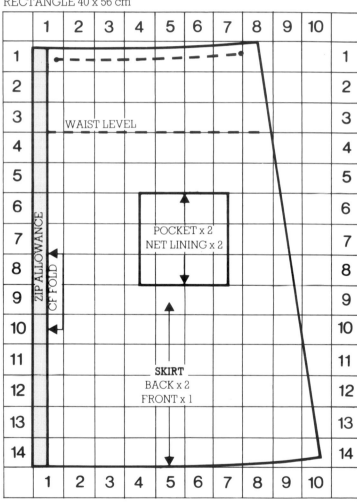

Order of making

(See sewing techniques 2, 15, 25, 12 and 6.)

1 Stitch shoulder seams of bodice and those of net lining.

2 Match lining to bodice and stitch round edges, leaving bottom open. Turn out.

3 Stitch side seams of skirt and press centre back turning allowance.

4 Make pockets, add frilling edge and stitch into position on skirt.

5 Gather skirt to fit bodice leaving 10 cm at each side seam to be hemmed and elasticated. (This is the part of the waistline between the front and back 'bibs'.)

6 Stitch skirt to bodice.

7 Turn and stitch hem.
Note Frilling may be used at hem if you prefer.

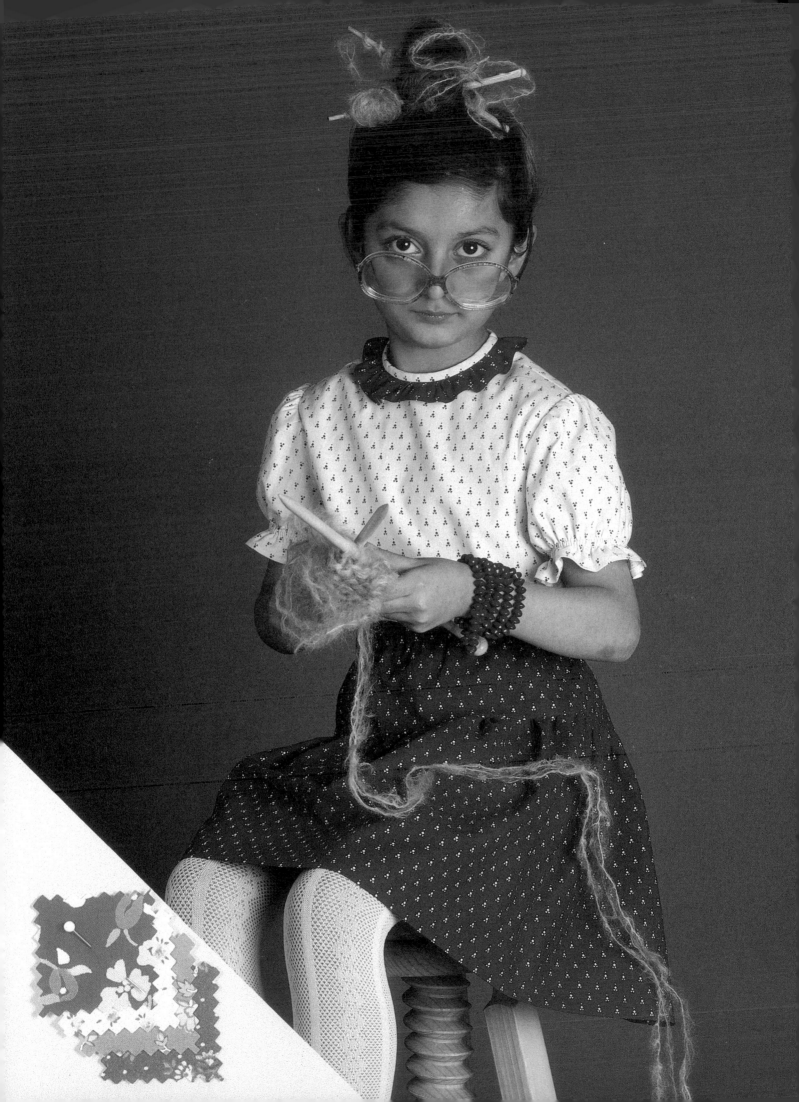

Velvet Dress

A special dress for special occasions is a must in every child's wardrobe. The ideal fabric is 100 per cent cotton velvet, which handles easily and looks good with very little pressing. Be sure to cut the fabric in one direction only to avoid 'shading'.

The neckline is trimmed with purchased frilling and bound. The sleeves, which can be long or short, are elasticated or frilled. A centre back zip fastens the garment. The contrast satin sash is cut on the cross to tie smoothly into a bow behind the waist. Recommended fabrics for the dress also include velveteen and non-stretch velour.

Order of making

(See sewing techniques 5, 2, 25, 7, 11, 21, 6 and 17.)

1 Stitch darts.

2 Stitch shoulder seams.

3 Stitch frilling to neckline and bind neck.

4 Gather sleeve heads to fit armholes.

5 Stitch side seams of bodice. Stitch sleeve seams.

6 Stitch sleeves into armholes.

7 Turn a small hem on sleeves and insert elastic to fit wrists comfortably.

8 Stitch side seams of skirt and centre back seam from base of zip opening to bottom edge of skirt.

9 Gather skirt to fit bodice and stitch together.

10 Turn and stitch hem.

11 Make a contrast or matching sash.

To fit ages 2(3-4)5   (Sizes 6–11 are on pages 56 and 58)

RECTANGLE 36 x 28 cm

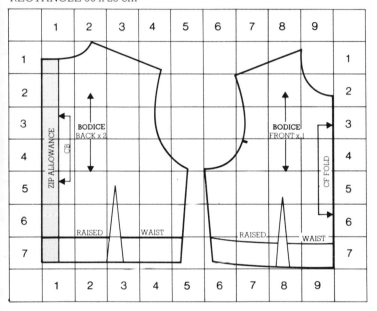

RECTANGLE 32 x 44 cm

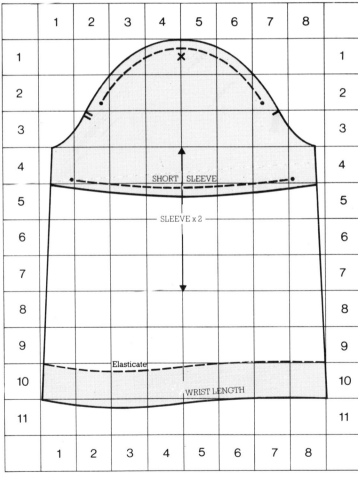

RECTANGLE 90 x 35 cm

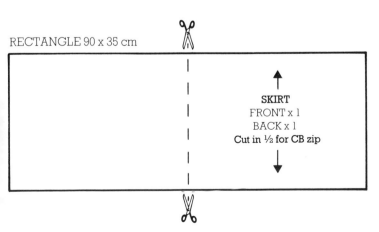

93

Victorian-style Pinafore

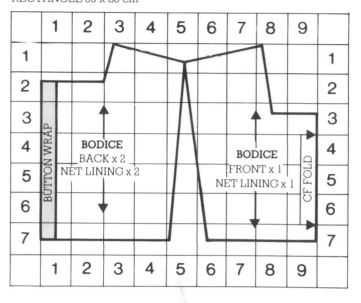

This high-waisted pinafore made in broderie anglais is a very attractive addition to any of the dresses. The bodice and pockets are lined with fine net to emphasize the pattern of the fabric. The pinafore buttons down the back of the bodice, leaving the skirt loose. Frilling emphasizes the position of the pockets. Recommended fabrics include broderie anglais and organza.

The dress pattern can be taken from the diagram on page 56 or 58, the only difference being that the sleeve is gathered near the bottom edge to form a frill. Recommended fabrics include cotton, lawn and pure silk.

Order of making

(See sewing techniques 2, 15, 25, 12 and 6.)

1 Stitch shoulder seams of bodice and those of net lining.

2 Match lining to bodice and stitch round edges, leaving bottom open. Turn out.

3 Stitch side seams of skirt and press centre back turning allowance.

4 Make pockets, add frilling edge and stitch into position on skirt.

5 Gather skirt to fit bodice leaving 10 cm at each side seam to be hemmed and elasticated. (This is the part of the waistline between the front and back 'bibs'.)

6 Stitch skirt to bodice.

7 Turn and stitch hem.
Note Frilling may be used at hem if you prefer.

RECTANGLE 40 x 56 cm

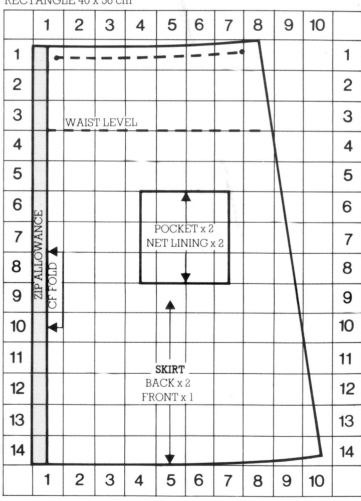

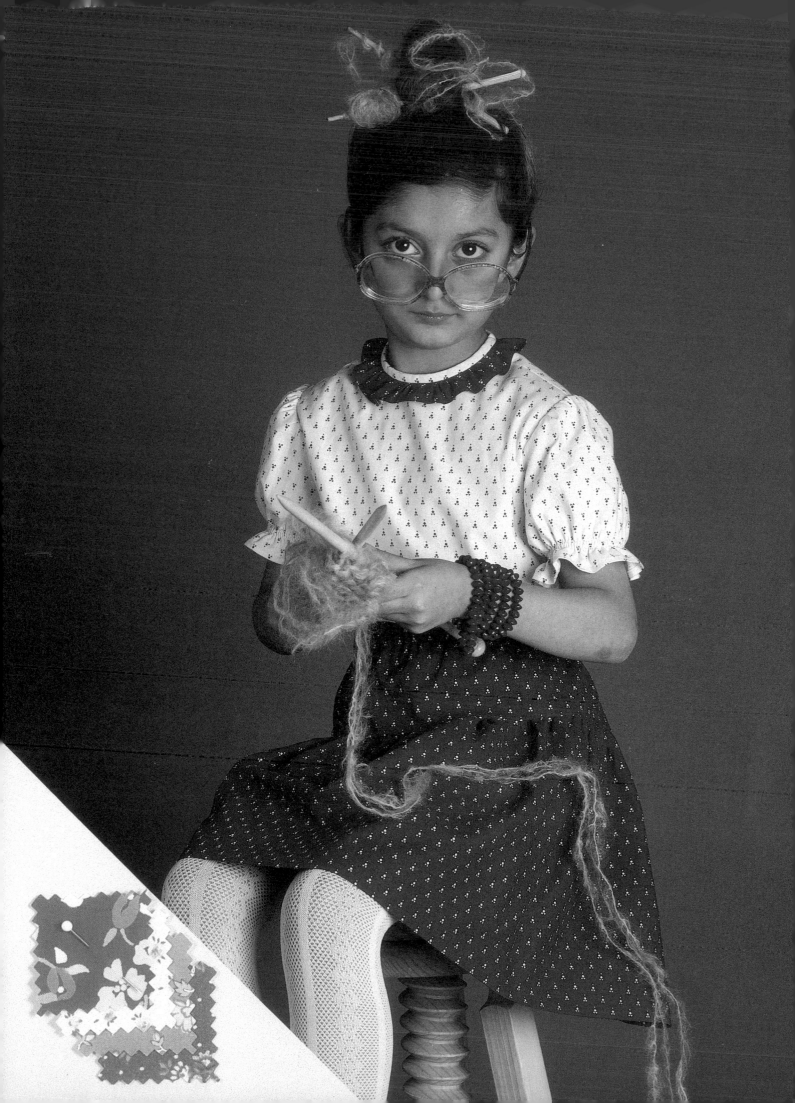

Frilled Blouse and Tiered Skirt

For the growing child a skirt and blouse is a very useful outfit; it can look exactly like a dress, but not have the disadvantage of a fixed waistline. Mix-and-match fabric, such as we have used in the photograph, makes a stylish combination. The skirt is cut in two tiers with the top hemmed and elasticated. The pattern and instructions are on page 52.

The blouse has a contrast frill that is bound to the neckline, and puffed sleeves elasticated above the hem to continue the frilled effect. The back fastens with buttons.

This outfit can be made in any woven fabric, but avoid large checks.

Order of making

(See sewing techniques 2, 25, 1, 7, 11, 6 and 18.)

1 Stitch shoulder seams.

2 Press back fold line of button wrap.

3 Attach frilling and bind neckline.

4 Gather sleeve heads to fit armholes.

5 Stitch side seams of blouse. Stitch sleeve seams.

6 Elasticate bottom of sleeves. Hem sleeves.

7 Stitch sleeves to armholes.

8 Turn and stitch hem.

9 Make buttonholes and attach buttons to centre back.

To fit ages 2(3-4)5
RECTANGLE 40 x 36 cm

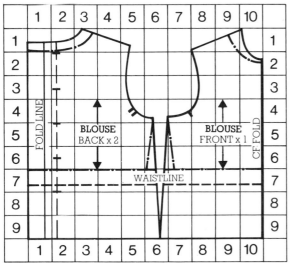

KEY ———·——·——
Cutting line for bolero blouse on page 52

To fit ages 4(5-6-7)8
RECTANGLE 44 x 44 cm

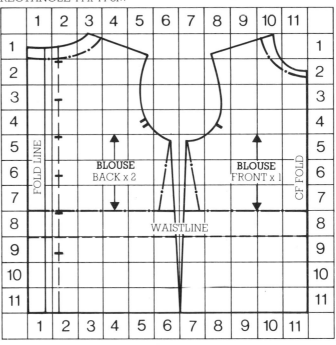

To fit ages 8(9-10)11
RECTANGLE 52 x 52 cm

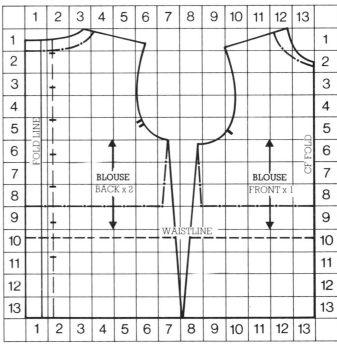

To fit all sizes
RECTANGLE 44 x 24 cm

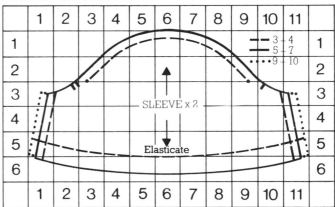

Pedal Pushers

Made from the basic trouser pattern on page 50, these pedal pushers are popular with girls of all ages. They have an elasticated waist and shaped side seams, but each leg can be cut as one piece if you prefer. As a fashion detail, you can make side splits by leaving open the bottom 10 cm of each side seam. Recommended fabrics include denim, gabardine and worsted.

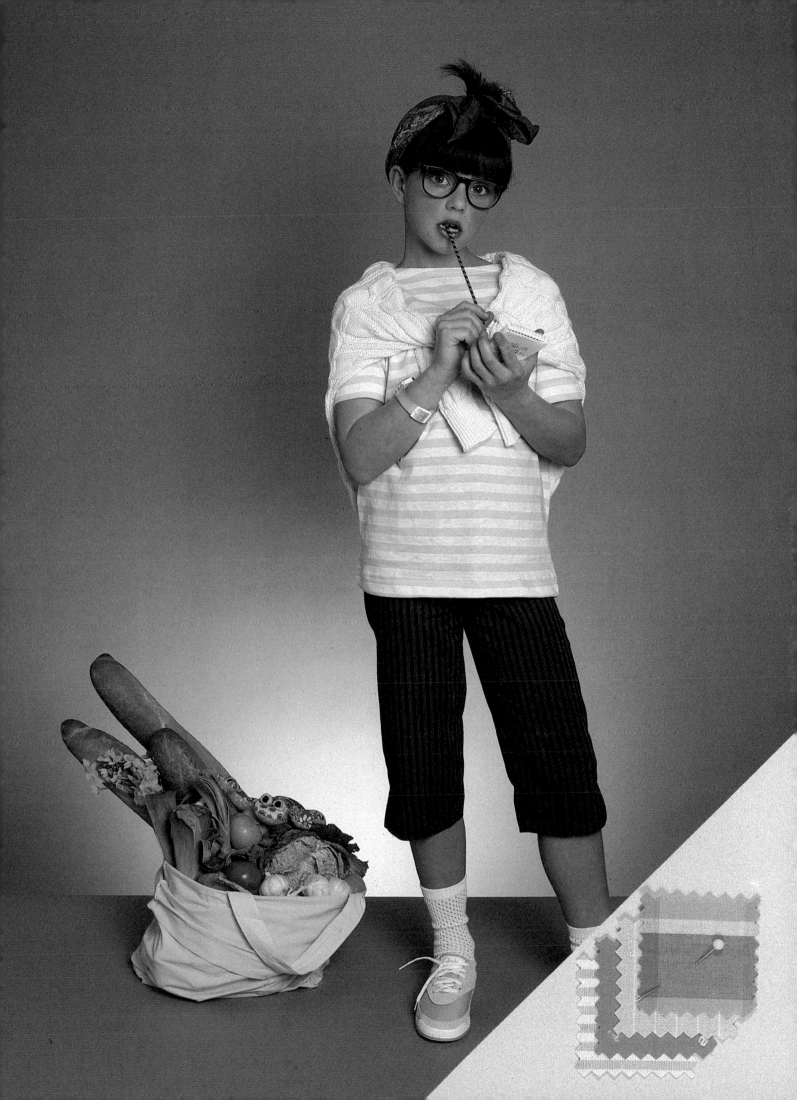

Elasticated Skirt

This is the easiest of all skirts to make. It does not need a pattern and the sewing is absolutely basic. Follow steps 1 – 5 for success every time.

1 Choose a fabric that is soft enough to gather well.

2 Make a note of the waist measurement required.

3 Make a note of the finished length required.

4 Draw a rectangle. Allow 6 cm to fold over for the elastic and 5 cm for the hem.

5 Make the pockets to any size you like and stitch them on the front or sides of the skirt.

Order of making

(See sewing techniques 15, 2, 11 and 6.)

1 Make pockets and stitch in place.

2 Stitch centre back seam.

3 Turn top hem, stitch and insert a length of elastic 2.5 cm shorter than the waist size.

4 Turn and stitch hem.

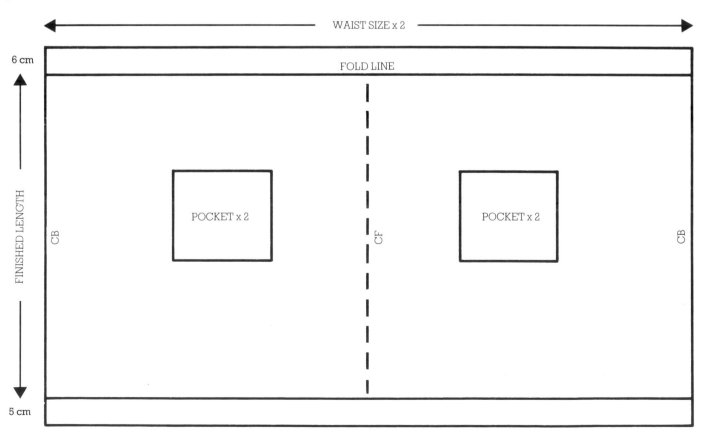

Wrapover Dress

The wrapover front of this dress is a very attractive fashion detail, particularly if the fabric is cut on the cross. It has long ends that tie behind the back and is fully lined with a fine washable lining. It is stitched into the shoulder and side seams but remains loose at the waist. The waistline darts are optional. The neckline is bound and the dress fastens with a centre back zip.

Order of making

(See sewing techniques 24, 2, 7, 11, 21, 3 and 6.)

1 Stitch wrapover fronts to lining and turn right sides out, leaving side seams open.

2 Place wrapover pieces on front bodice and tack shoulders and side seams together.

3 Stitch shoulder seams and side seams.

4 Bind neckline.

5 Gather sleeve heads to fit armholes and stitch sleeve seams.

6 Stitch sleeves into armholes.

7 Hem sleeves and elasticate about 3 cm from bottom to form wrist frill.

8 Stitch side seams of skirt. Stitch centre back seam from base of zip to bottom edge.

Note Before gathering skirt check fit of bodice to decide if waist darts are desirable.

9 Gather skirt to fit bodice.

10 Stitch skirt to bodice, ensuring that wrapover is not stitched into seam.

11 Insert zip.

12 Turn and stitch hem.

To fit ages 8-11 (age 10 illustrated)
RECTANGLE 48 x 40 cm

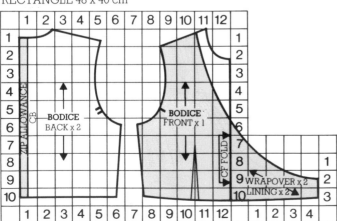

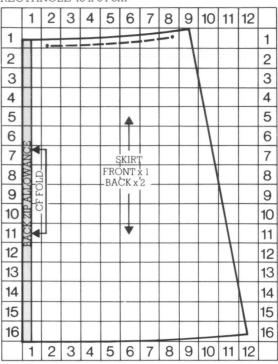

RECTANGLE 48 x 64 cm

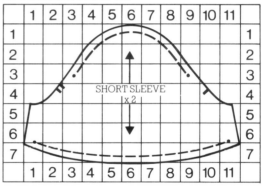

RECTANGLE 44 x 28 cm

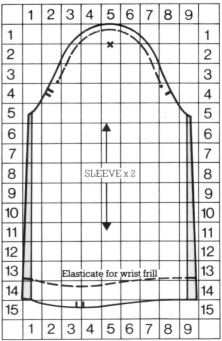

RECTANGLE 36 x 60 cm

Costume Pattern

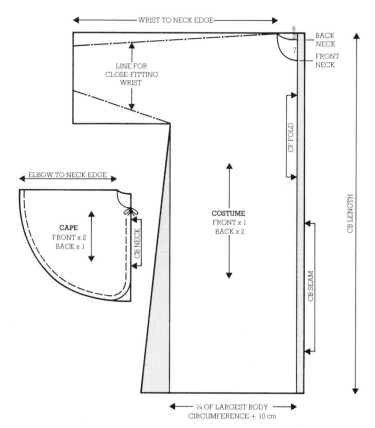

Every child at some time comes home asking for a costume for a school show or church play. Even if you've never sewn before, don't panic! The garments in our Nativity photograph are all based on a simple T-shaped pattern with a head opening. Once you have this made, you can ring the changes for different characters by using all kinds of accessories.

Our Nativity costumes were entirely made from curtain fabric which is warm and has enough weight to hang nicely. The neckline is bound and has ties to fasten behind the neck. Curtain shops frequently have remnants in glorious colours and I have often made exotic accessories from evening dresses, hats and costume jewellery picked up at jumble sales.

This simple pattern can form the basis for a host of costumes, and may even be used for a choir robe. There are two sleeve variations and a cuff may be added to the narrow version. Additional flare may be added to the garment by cutting on the outer line at the side seams.

For a professional finish to the choir robe, you might like to add the circular shoulder cape in a contrasting colour. Recommended fabrics are knitted polyester or Crimplene for the robe, and polyester cotton for the cape.

Costume

Order of making
(See sewing techniques 2, 1 and 6.)

1 Stitch centre back seam, leaving an opening at top for head.

2 Stitch shoulder seams.

3 Bind neckline, leaving long ends to tie behind the neck.

4 Stitch side seams and sleeve seams in one operation.

5 Turn and stitch hem.

Cape

Order of making
(See sewing techniques 6, 1 and 13.)
1 Measure from neck edge to elbow and use this measurement as radius of your garment. (The back is placed on a fold of the fabric.)

2 Machine hem all outer edges.

3 Bind neckline, leaving long ends to tie at front. A collar can be added if required.

Sewing techniques

There are many different ways of doing things in dressmaking, some easier than others, but all of them acceptable if you like the finished result and find it relatively easy to do. If you find something especially difficult, try another method; it can be particularly useful to look at ready-made clothes as manufacturers can teach the home dressmaker a few quick tips.

As you will see in the following pages, I have not used many different sewing techniques in this book; most of them are very easy to do, and you will certainly find this to be true with a little practice.

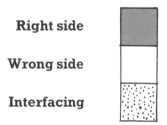

Right side

Wrong side

Interfacing

1 Binding

Preparing bias strips

a Fold fabric at right angles, so that edge A-B is straight up and down the fabric, and edge B-C is straight across the fabric.

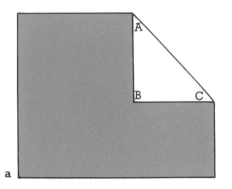

b Mark out strips about 3 cm wide (for single binding) or 4 cm wide (for double binding). Cut them carefully to keep edges straight.

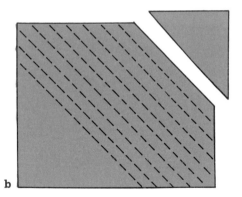

Joining bias strips

c Place fabric right sides together, angled as shown above. Open and clip edges straight.

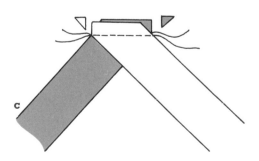

Single binding

d Using a small seam, stitch one edge of binding to right side of garment.

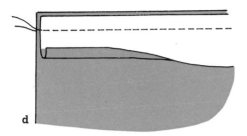

e Bring binding over to wrong side of fabric, turn under a small hem and handstitch into place.

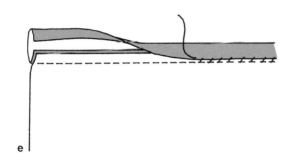

Concave binding

f On inward curving edges binding should be slightly eased to right side of garment when first stitching is done. Finish as shown in step e.

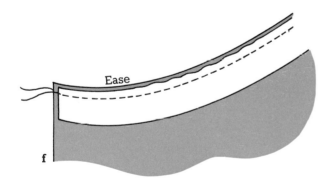

Convex binding

g On outward curving edges binding should be stretched slightly when first stitching is done. Finish as shown in step e.

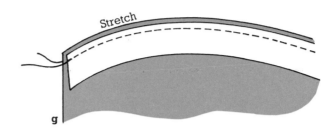

One-step binding

h Bias binding can be bought in a large range of colours and is ready-folded for use. You can make your own folded and pressed binding look like this with a special gadget available from good haberdashers. The strips of bias are passed through the device and come out folded and ready for pressing. To attach this sort of binding tack it over edge of garment, making sure that both sides are secured.

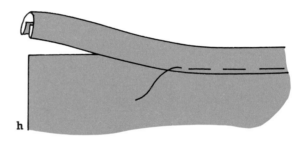

i Carefully machine through both sides at same time.

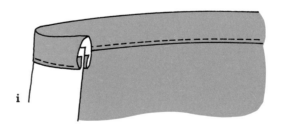

Double binding

j Fold binding strip in half lengthways, wrong sides together. Using a small seam, stitch edges to right side of garment.

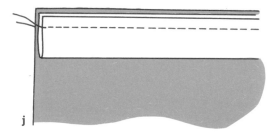

k Fold double binding over to wrong side and handstitch as in step e.

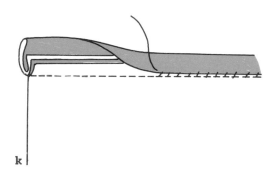

Easy binding

l Overlock (zig-zag stitch) one edge of binding strip. Making a small seam, stitch unzig-zagged edge to right side of fabric. Note how binding is wrapped round main fabric for neatly finished ends.

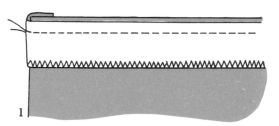

m Fold binding over to wrong side and tack or pin from right side in 'ditch' of first seam. Use a zipper foot to stitch accurately in this 'ditch' on right side of garment.

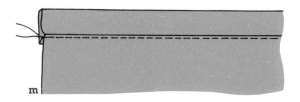

Bound neckline with tie ends

Prepare enough binding to go round the neck and leave long ends to tie. Try to make any joins in the binding come to a shoulder seam or to the centre back neck.

n Starting from centre back neck, position and stitch one edge of binding to neckline.

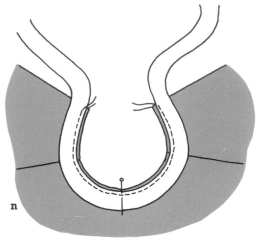

o For tie ends, fold binding in half lengthways (right sides together) and stitch up to neck edge.

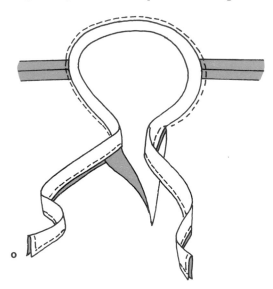

p Push tie ends through to right side. This produces 'rouleau' ties.

Finish the neckline by handstitching binding to inside.

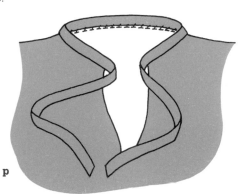

2 Seams

Open seam

a A seam allowance of 1.5 cm is standard and you should practise judging this distance on spare fabric. Otherwise tack or pin seam *before* machining.

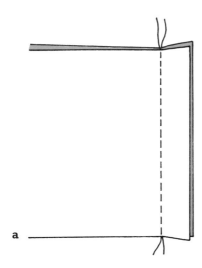

Eased seam

b Very often one seam edge is longer than the edge to which it must be sewn. The longer edge should be gently gathered or eased to fit the shorter edge *before* machining.

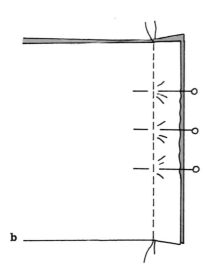

French seam

c This technique is recommended for fine and delicate fabrics that fray and where the seams can be seen. Stitch half normal seam allowance, *but with wrong sides together.* Trim seam down to a minimum.

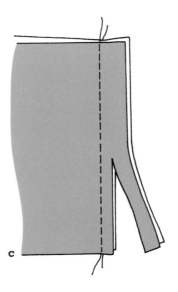

d Fold fabric right sides together and stitch another seam, completely enclosing first seam.

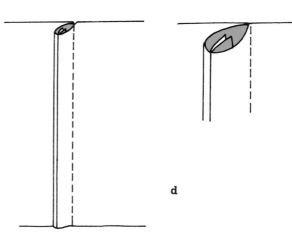

Lap and fell seam

e This is a seam used for reversible and quilted fabrics. With wrong sides together, stitch a normal seam. Trim *one side only* of the seam to a minimum. Fold remaining seam edge over trimmed edge, turn it under and stitch again on right side to secure finished seam. Contrast thread can highlight this method.

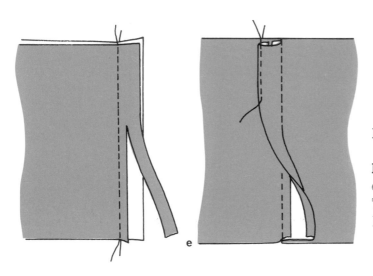

Pinked seams

f If you have a pair of pinking shears you can trim seam edges to help stop fraying. As an additional help to stop fraying you can stitch along seam edges *before* pinking, but be careful not to cut stitching when you trim.

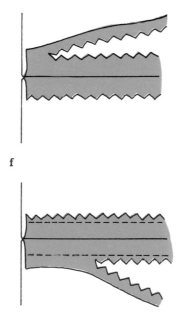

Zig-zagged seam

g This is by far the quickest method if you have a zig-zag facility on your machine. I find it useful to zig-zag as many edges as possible *before* I stitch the seams.

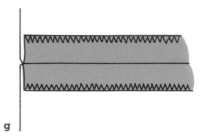

Bound seam

h Unlined coats look much neater inside if the seam edges are bound, particularly in a contrasting colour. This technique also strengthens the edges (see Binding on page 106).

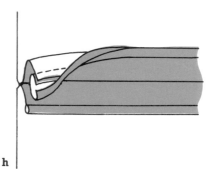

3. Zips

a Check your zip length against your garment, and mark where base of zip finishes. With right sides together stitch seam of garment from base of zip opening to bottom edge of garment.

Edge-to-edge method

b Press seam open (including part for zip) and tack zip in edge-to-edge position as illustrated. You may find this easier to do if you tack zip opening in fabric *before* tacking zip into position. Machine (or hand-sew) into place, stitching base of zip in either of the ways shown. Remove tacking.

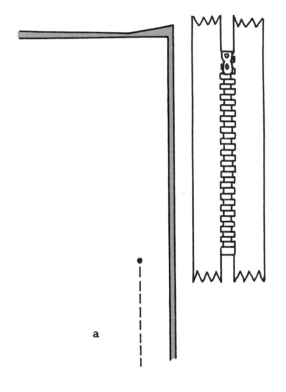

a

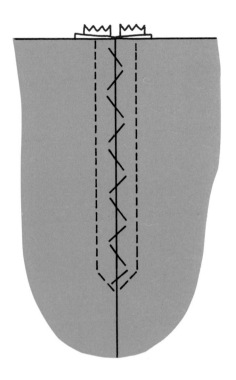

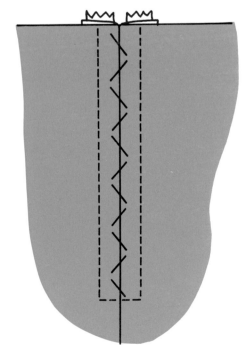

b

Lapped method

c Prepare seam opening as described in step a. Using a zipper foot on your machine, stitch from base of zip to top of zip, close to zip teeth.

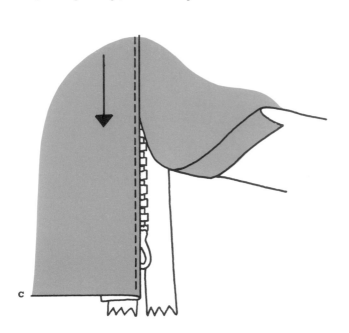

e Using a left-handed zipper foot, or swinging a fixed zipper foot to a left-hand position, machine across base of zip, turn and stitch up remaining side.

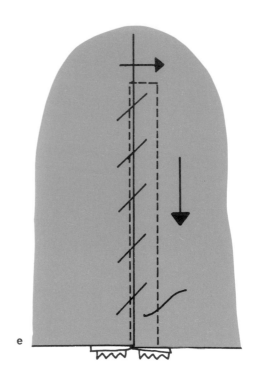

d Bring remaining edge over to cover zip and tack into place.

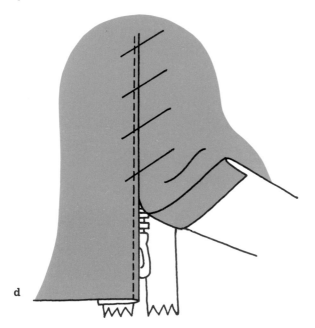

4. Facings

a Stitch shoulder seams of neck facings and neaten outer edges (see seam finishes, page 110). Then stitch facings to neckline. Stitch down facings on centre back seam line.

b Clip curved neckline seam so facings fold smoothly to inside of garment.

c Turn facings to inside of garment and stitch to seam allowance from the inside. This stitching does not show on outside and helps to stop facings rolling outwards.

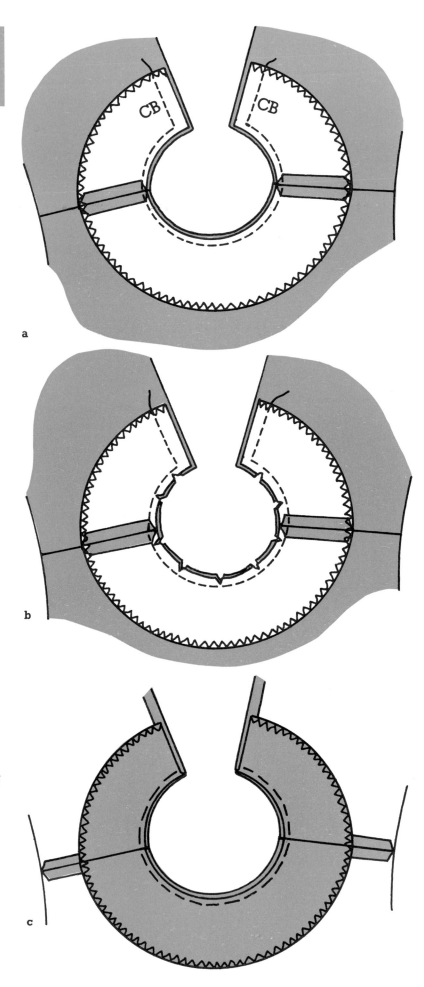

Blouse/jacket facings (front or back opening)

Interfacing should be used to strengthen front edges and to support buttonholes. A lightweight fusible interfacing is recommended, and this should be pressed to the facings after cutting out.

d Stitch shoulder seams of facings. With right sides together, place facings on garment. Stitch all round outer edge. This effectively encases a collar or any neck trimming you are using.

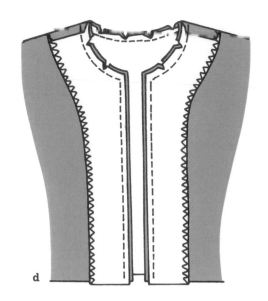

e Turn facings to inside of garment and stitch to seam allowance from the inside as illustrated. This stitching does not show on outside and helps to stop facings rolling outwards. Neaten raw edges of facings by hemming, zig-zagging or binding.

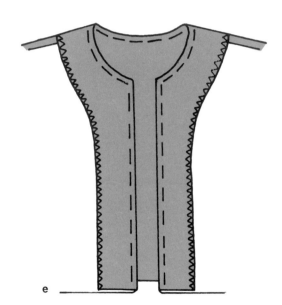

f Handcatch facings to inside of garment.

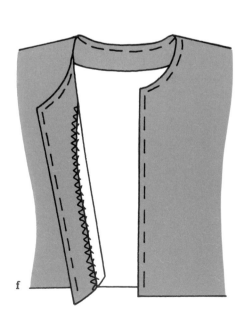

114

5. Darts

a Fold and tack the dart, then stitch from widest part to point of dart. Reverse stitch to secure ends. Press dart in this position, before opening it out for step b.

a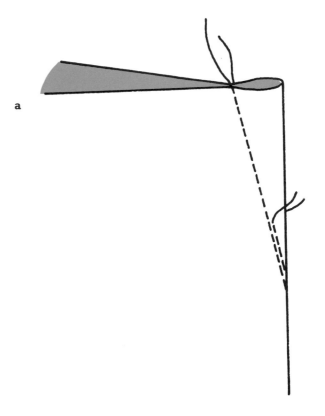

b Position dart evenly over stitching line and carefully press. Use brown paper under edges to avoid marking through to right side of fabric.

b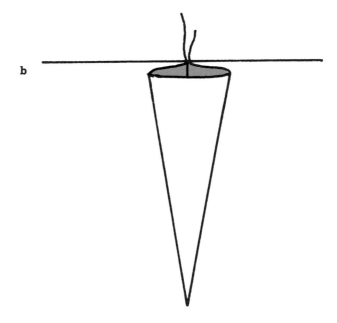

6. Hems

a Always level hems from the floor upwards, using a long ruler or piece of dowelling with a rubber band twisted round it. The band can be pushed up and down to the required length. Place pins horizontally and at regular intervals as you move round the hem.

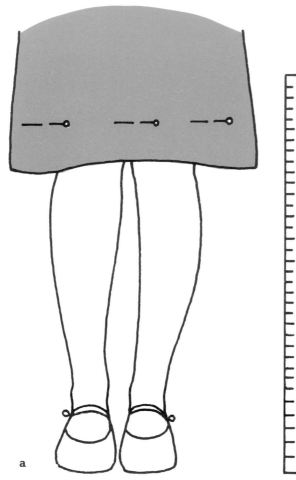

b Fold up hem and tack a short distance up from bottom edge. Remove pins. Trim hem to a regular depth and neaten top edge.

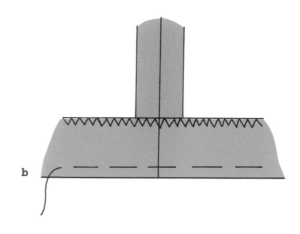

c Flared hems should not be too deep. They need to be eased on curves, and you can do this by placing pins at regular intervals and keeping a little fullness between them.

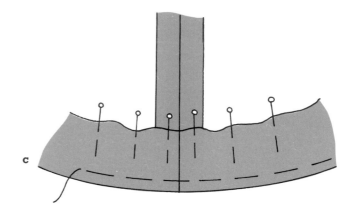

d There are many ways of stitching a hem, including machining, which I think always looks better than a badly handsewn hem. You should practise hand-sewing and find which method you prefer. *Catch-stitch* is worked with the stitches showing and is a very secure hem.

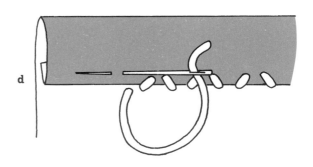

e *Concealed catch-stitch* is worked inside and below top of hem, and should not under any circumstances be pulled tight. It can be successfully used on stretch fabrics.

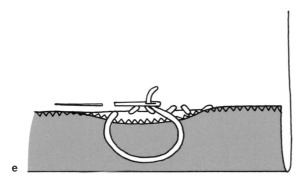

f *Bound hems* have binding attached to the top of the hem and are then handstitched to garment.

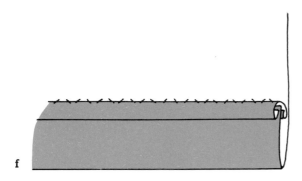

g *Blind hemming* gives a very neat finish on the wrong side of garment.

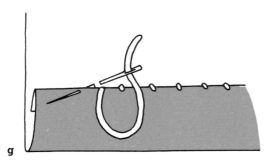

7. Sleeves

Set-in sleeves

a *Open seam method:* With small garments, such as children's clothes, it is much easier to put in the sleeves *before* you stitch the side seams. Make sure you recognize the front and back of sleeves so they are placed in garment correctly. Any ease or gather in sleeve head should be done *before* you tack sleeve into armhole.

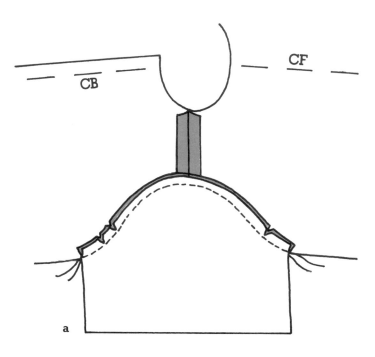

b Stitch side seams and sleeve seams in one operation.

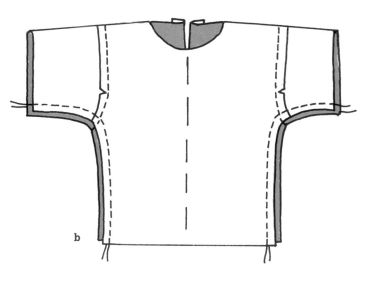

c *Closed seam method:* If you set sleeves into garment after side seams and sleeve seams have been stitched, pin sleeve to garment, as illustrated, using more pins where gathers have to be positioned.

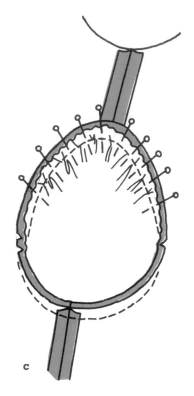

There are various types of raglan sleeve: one piece with a dart, one piece without a dart and (particularly useful if you're short of fabric) cut as two pieces with a seam down the middle and the dart edges taking the shape of the shoulder.

Darted raglan sleeves

d Stitch dart. (This forms shoulder line.)

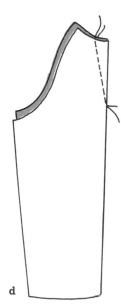

e Cut away inside top of dart to reduce bulk at neckline.

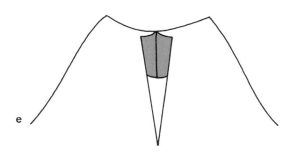

Raglan sleeves

f Raglan sleeves (with or without a dart) are stitched to front and back of garment.

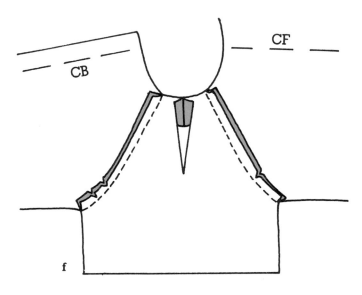

g As with set-in sleeves, side seams and sleeve seams are stitched in one operation.

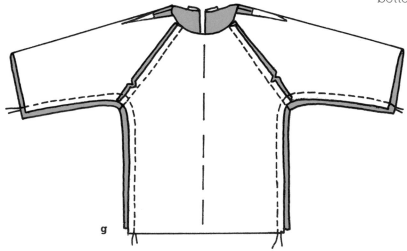

Gathered sleeve head

h Sew a running stitch just above seam line and evenly gather sleeve head to fit armhole. *Do this before garment side seams are stitched.*

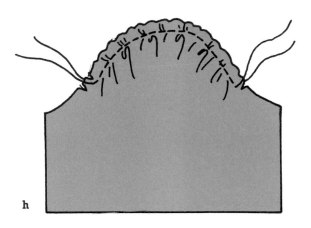

i The bottom of a gathered sleeve may have elastic inserted in hem to form a puffed sleeve, or a little way up to leave a frilled edge.

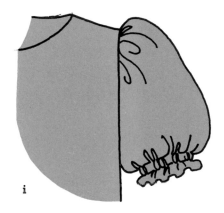

j A cuffed band may be added to a gathered sleeve bottom (see technique 9).

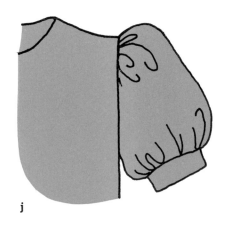

k The bottom of a gathered sleeve left loose and hemmed gives a cape effect.

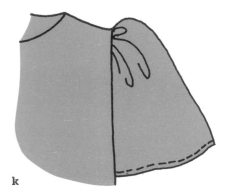

k

l Shirring elastic used above the sleeve hem gives a 'pie-crust' frill. Some shops sell elastic webbing in different widths. This gives a shirred effect when stitched into place and may be easier to do.

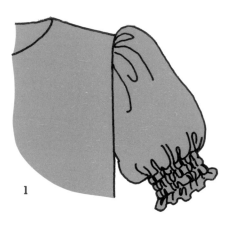

l

m The sleeve armhole can be neatened with a machine zig-zag stitch or very soft binding.

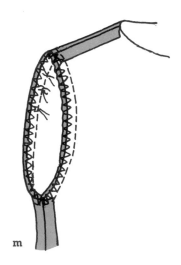

m

8. Cuffs

Cuffs are made and attached in exactly the same way as waistbands (see technique 10). The sleeve may be prepared for them in the following ways.

Open cuffs

a Sleeves with cuffs need an opening in the sleeve to allow it to go over the hand. The simplest opening is the small stitched hem indicated by notches on the pattern. Clip seam allowance between these notches.

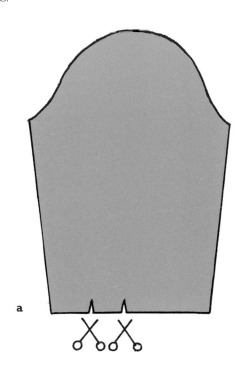

b Turn and stitch small hem.

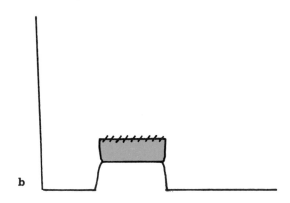

c Gather sleeve to fit cuff and attach as illustrated. When buttoned this sleeve opening forms a pleat.

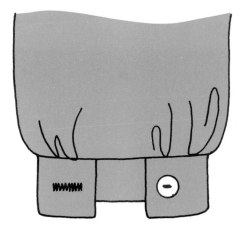

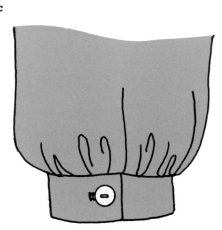

d A faced sleeve opening has a small piece of fabric, preferably cut on the cross, stitched to right side of sleeve over notched back opening position. Cut up centre of stitching through both fabrics.

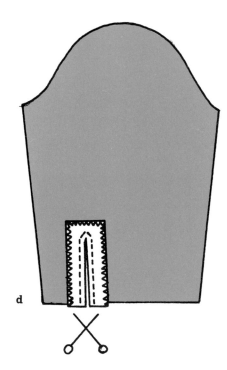

e Turn facing to inside of sleeve. Handstitch round facing or machine stitch close to slashed opening. When buttoned this gives an opening at back of sleeve.

Continuous cuffs
f Stitch sleeve seam. Press seam open then turn and stitch a deep hem.

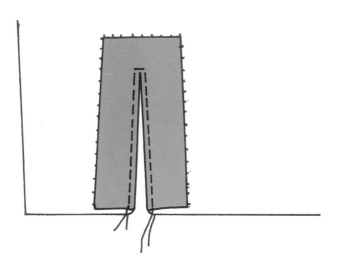

e

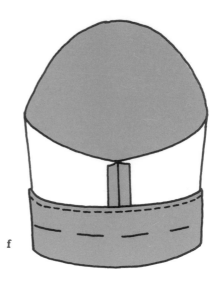

f

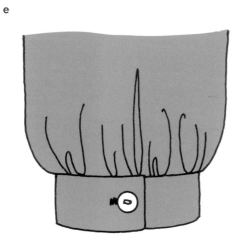

g Fold cuff up on right side of garment.

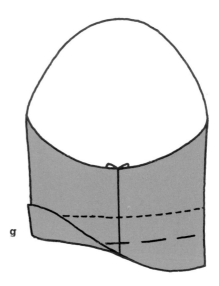

g

9. Stretch wrist, waist and ankle bands

1 In woven or non-stretch fabrics you must gather garment edge *before* attaching band.
2 In stretch fabrics garment should be gathered a little to reduce its size, then the band stretched slightly as it is sewn to garment.

  If you use a velour fabric, or any other that has a pile, you must check that it runs in the same direction on the band as on the garment.

a Fold fabric in half widthways and stitch seam to make a circle.

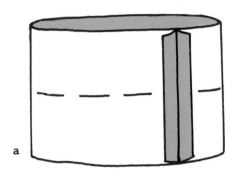

b Turn band to right side.

c Position seam of band to a seam on garment, preferably in the least seen position. Pin and stitch band to garment.

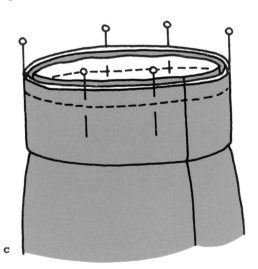

Note If garment edge is bigger than band, there are two solutions:

d Neaten stitched edge, preferably with a zig-zag stitch. In stretch fabrics it is important that seam stretches to get garment on and off.

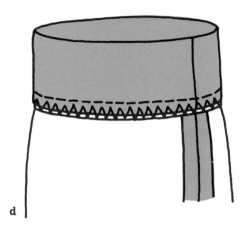

e The finished cuff.

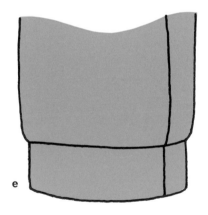

10. Waistbands

There are no patterns for waistbands in this book.

a Use special waistband-width interfacing and cut a length to waist size plus 6.5 cm (1.5 cm at one end and 5 cm at the other). Iron this length on to fabric *before* cutting out to edges of interfacing.

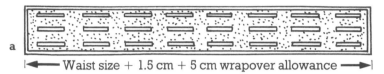

Waist size + 1.5 cm + 5 cm wrapover allowance

b Fold band lengthways right sides together and stitch ends as illustrated. Clip end of wrapover edge.

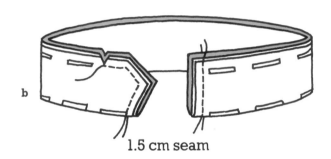

1.5 cm seam

c Turn band to right side.

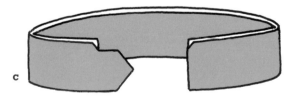

d Stitch one edge of waistband to skirt.

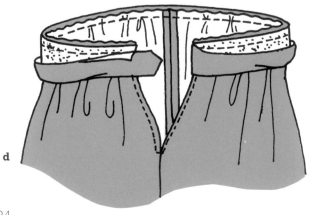

e Turn remaining edge under and handstitch to garment. Attach hooks and eyes or button and buttonhole to fasten.

Note Cuffs are made in exactly the same way as waistbands.

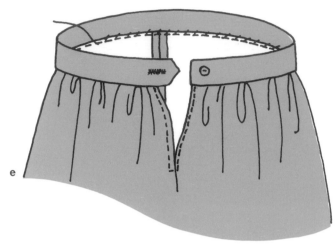

Wrapover skirt waistband

f Calculate length of waistband required after skirt has been tried on with wrapover tacked down centre front line. Follow steps a to e to make and attach waistband.

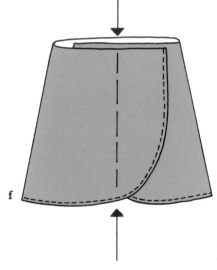

g To fasten skirt, add a button and buttonhole at either end of wrapover.

11. Elasticated waists and hems

This is the most successful way of finishing waists on children's clothes because it does away with critical fitting problems and can be easily adjusted for comfort.

a Fold line for elasticated hem is marked on patterns as a dotted line.

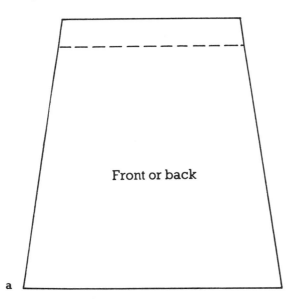

Front or back

a

b Stitch skirt or trouser (except hems). Turn top hem to inside of the garment and stitch, leaving a small gap unstitched (preferably over a seam) to thread elastic through.

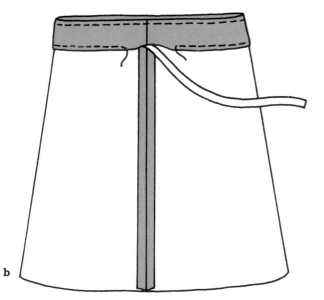

b

c Skirts in soft fabric look very pretty with a 'pie-crust' frill at the top. To achieve this effect, stitch a row of machining a little way down from top edge and use narrower elastic.

The length and tightness of the elastic should be determined by trying it round the child's waist *before* threading it through casing. Remember to add at least 3 cm for overlapped join.

c

d Hand or machine stitch opening left for elastic.

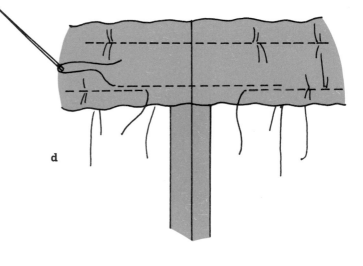

d

12. Partially elasticated waist

Victorian-style apron

a When bib top is stitched to skirt there is gap left at side seams.

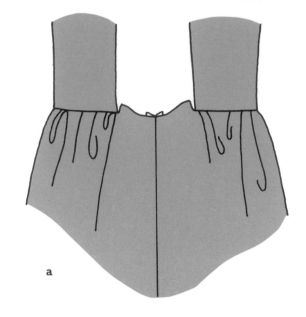

b Using seam allowance, turn and stitch this as a hem.

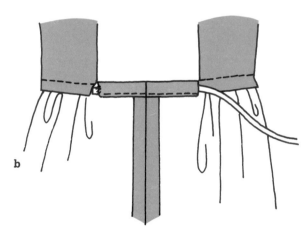

c Thread elastic through hem to gather sides as required.

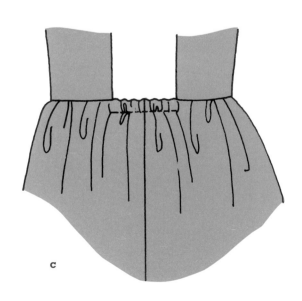

13. Collars

There are two main methods for making collars.
1 Cut in two pieces, the fabric is placed right sides together with interfacing on top. The outer edge is stitched as shown in step a. Trim and layer the seam after stitching. Turn to the right side and press.
2 Some collars are cut on a fold of the fabric so outer edge does not need stitching. Place right sides together and stitch ends. Turn to right side and press.

a All collars should be made up with a lightweight interfacing to help keep the shape and add crispness. They also lie and fit better if the *under collar* is cut on the crossway grain of the fabric. Try to do this whenever possible.

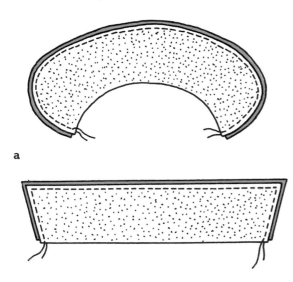

b Pin or tack under collar to the two centre front points and then stitch.

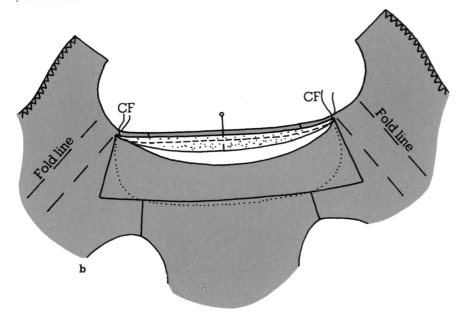

c Neaten raw edges of bodice facings, except neck edge, and fold back on to right side of garment. Stitch facings and top collar to garment.

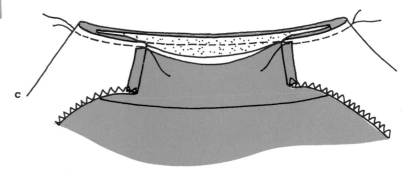

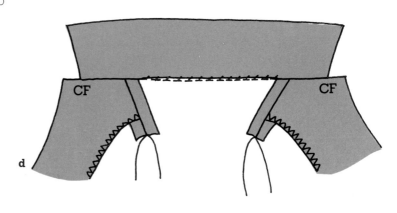

d Close collar by handstitching along seam line, or machine across edge using a zig-zag finish.
   The neatened edge of facings can be handstitched to shoulder seams.

127

e The finished collar, used with a front-opening garment, can either be fastened right up to the neck, or the buttoning can start lower to form a collar and rever.

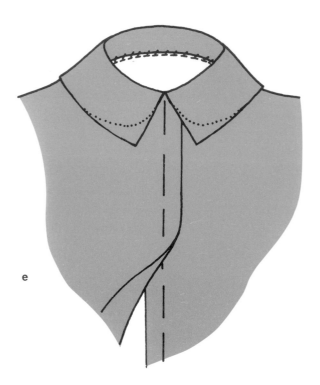

Sailor collar

f Place right sides together and stitch round outer edges as illustrated. Trim seams and clip corners before turning to right side.

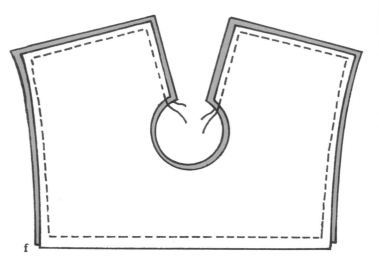

g With back seam turned to inside of garment, stitch collar to neckline. Bind neckline (see page 108).

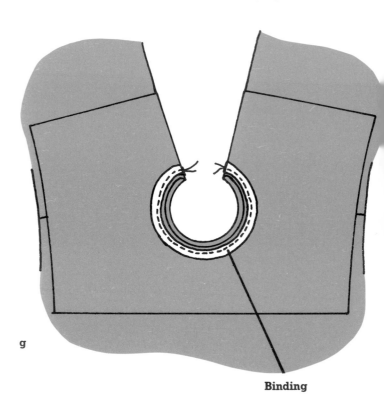

Binding

Note Step g is used for many collars and neck trimmings in the book. The binding may be in either matching or contrast fabric.

14. Hoods

Pramsuit hood

a This is made from a centre panel and two sides. Stitch as shown with right sides together.

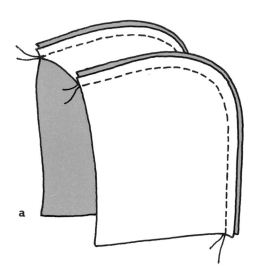

b Clip and press seams open. Lap and fell seams may be used on suitable fabric, or edges may be overlocked (zig-zagged). Turn and stitch front hem.

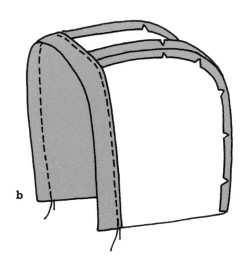

One-piece hood (for anorak and duffel coat)

c Fold fabric as indicated and stitch centre back seam. Press seam open.

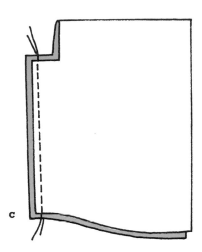

d Re-fold hood and stitch across remaining edge.

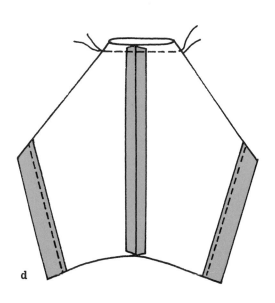

Two-piece hood

e Stitch centre seam with right sides together. Trim and press seams open.

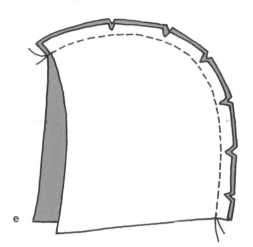

f Turn and stitch front hem.

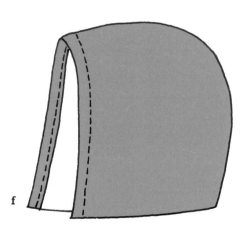

All hoods

g With right sides together, carefully position centre back and stitch hood to garment.

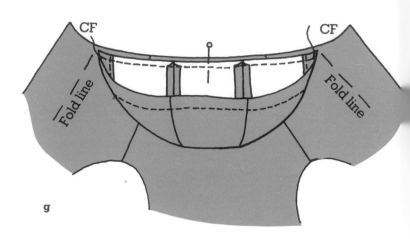

h Fold back the centre front facings and stitch as illustrated.

The neckline can either be bound or overlocked (zig-zagged).

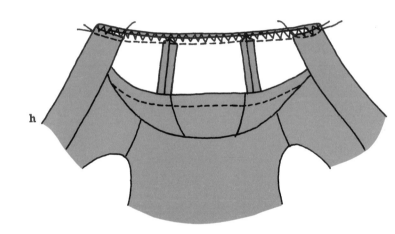

15. Pockets and pocket flaps

Patch pockets

a Place fabric and lining right sides together and stitch round edges, leaving an opening so pocket can be turned to right side. (The lining does not have to be in the same fabric as the garment.) Trim seam allowance and clip corners. Turn pocket to right side.

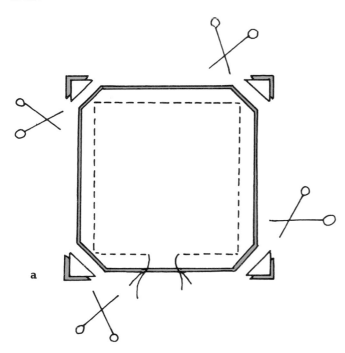

b Position pocket on garment and stitch into place, leaving top edge open. Reinforced stitching is recommended for corners.

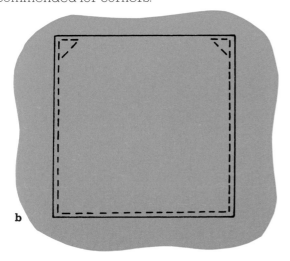

Bound pockets

c Binding is easier on curved edges. Bind round outer edge, then across top edge as illustrated. Position pocket on garment. Using a zipper foot stitch in the 'ditch' created by edge of binding.

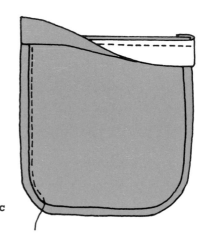

Side pockets

d Place fabric and lining right sides together and stitch round three edges as illustrated. Trim and clip seams. Turn to right side through open side seam.

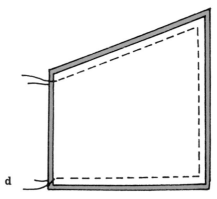

e Stitch pocket to garment as illustrated.

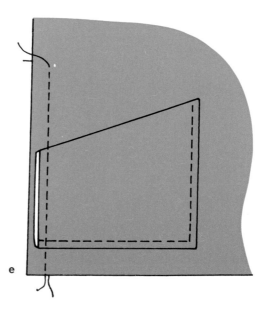

131

Inseam pockets

f With right sides together, stitch pocket pieces to each side seam as illustrated.

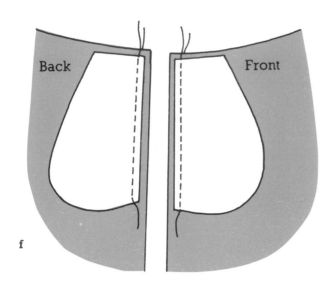

g Press out as shown.

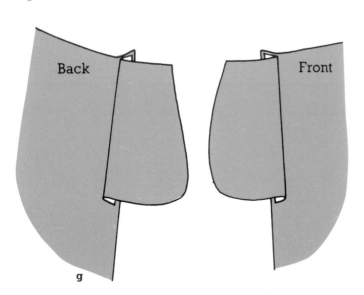

h With the right sides together, stitch side seam and pocket in one operation. Carefully clip seam below pocket and press open.

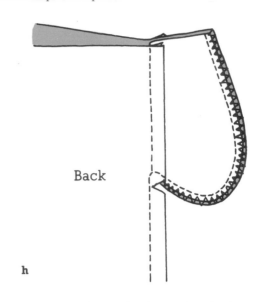

i Fold pockets to front of skirt and tack along waistline.

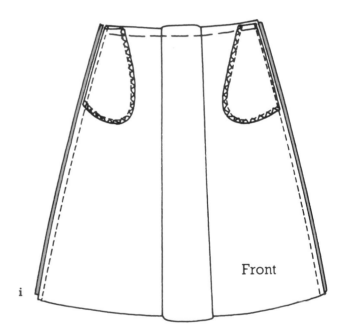

Pouch pocket

j Bind curved edges using contrast fabric for effect. Bind across top edge.

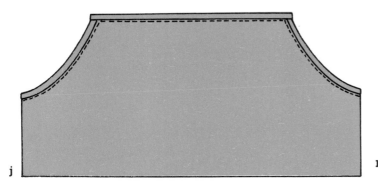

k Position pocket on completed front of bodice and stitch across top edge and at side seams.

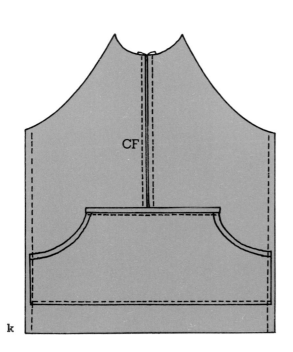

Note Ensure pocket is positioned with sufficient hem allowance at bottom to allow either elastic or cord to be threaded through.

Pocket flaps

l With right sides together stitch around edges as illustrated, leaving top edge open. Trim and clip seams.

m Turn flap to right side. Neaten remaining edge.

Note If this is to be a buttoned flap you will find it easier to make the buttonhole *before* stitching flap to garment.

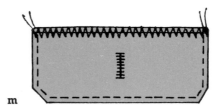

n Stitch flap into position over pocket. Add a button if required.

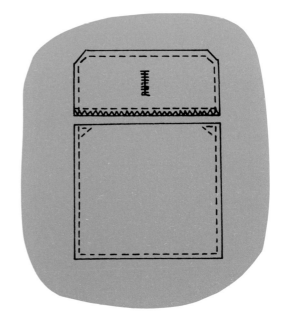

16. Popper fastenings

Poppers are a very useful method of fastening on all sorts of garments. They may be substituted for buttons on dresses, straps and cuffs. They are sold in packets of varying amounts, so try to decide in advance how many you will need. A special device for attaching these poppers is available from good haberdashers.

Dungarees

a Bind both sides of inside leg, or bind one side and hem the other.

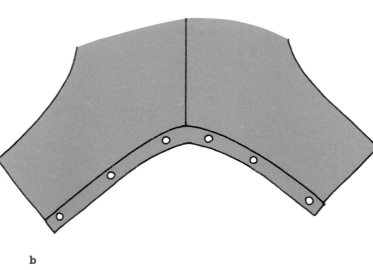

a

b Attach the first two poppers either side of crutch seam. Attach next two poppers to ankles. Evenly space remaining poppers along each leg to avoid gaping.

b

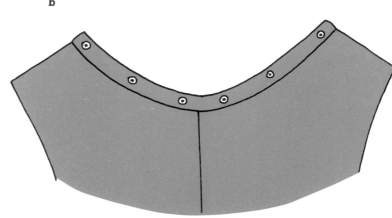

17. Shoulder straps

This technique is also suitable for making belts and sashes.

a With right sides together, stitch along folded strap.

b Turn strap to right side and press with seam in centre position, as illustrated.

c Check that straps are correct length for child and stitch into position on right side of bodice, allowing them to drop to sides ready for next sewing operation.

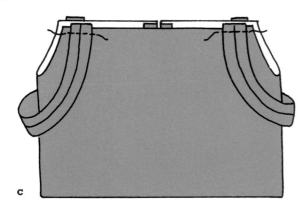

Enclosing straps on back buttoning garments

d *Full lining method:* With right side of lining facing right side of garment, stitch along top edges and down centre back seam lines. Clip and trim. Turn lining to inside of bodice and stitch the two fabrics together at bottom edge.

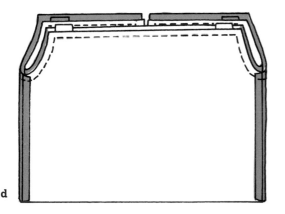

e *Top facing method:* Stitch facing to top edges and down centre back seam lines. Clip and trim. Turn and press facing to inside of garment.

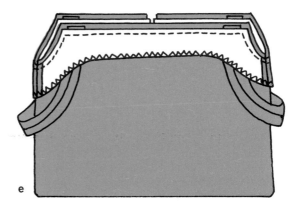

f If straps are cut in two pieces you can tie a bow or knot on the shoulders. This can be a useful option to allow for growth.

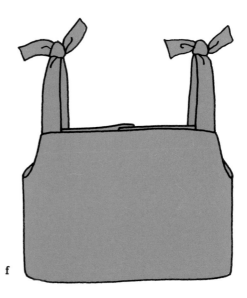

g Straps that cross over at back can be buttoned at front or back. Stitch only one end to garment, leaving other end neatened and ready for buttonhole.

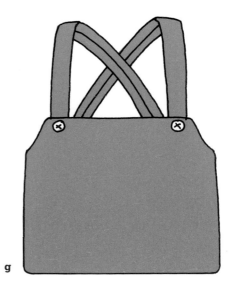

135

18. Buttons and buttonholes

Front and back buttoning

a The positioning of buttonholes depends very much upon the size of button you are using. The bigger the buttons, the wider apart the buttonholes should be. Ensure that the buttonholes are big enough to take the buttons without stretching and *always* work a trial buttonhole on scrap fabric before starting on garment. The position of buttons and buttonholes is determined by the centre front line of garment. It is recommended that you mark this with a tacking line.

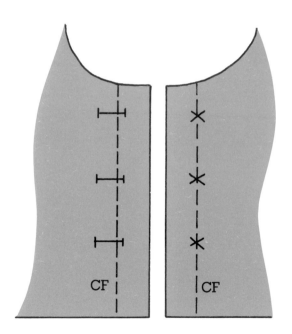

a

b Buttonholes may go either across or down the centre front line. Note carefully the positioning of these in the illustrations.

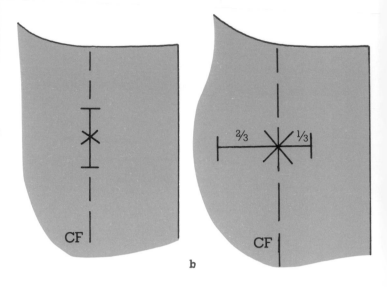

b

c Buttonholes can be worked by machine, or by hand, using a machine buttonhole thread.

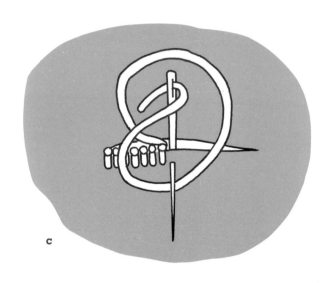

c

d Vertical buttonholes look better with squared ends.

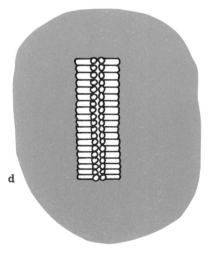

d

e Horizontal buttonholes may have one square end and one rounded end.

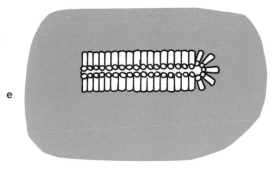

e

Side buttoning

f *Playsuit and Pinafore Dress:* Stitch side seam of trouser or skirt to base of waist extension as illustrated.

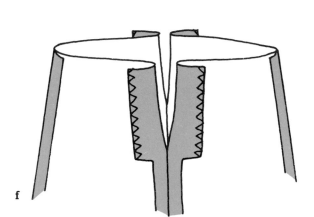

f

g Stitch and turn bottom of lined bodice as in a wrapover waistband fastening. Then stitch it to the skirt or trouser, with the folded back seam allowance stitched in with the waist line.

g

h The wrapover of the bodice now closes the seam and a button and buttonhole used to fasten the sides.

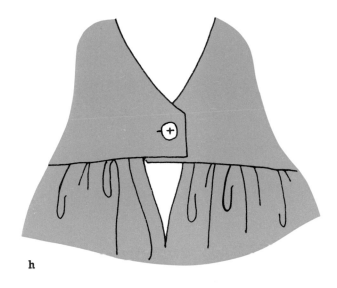

h

i *Sun dress:* Make and stitch straps as shown in 17 a, b and c. With right sides together, stitch facings to top of bodice.

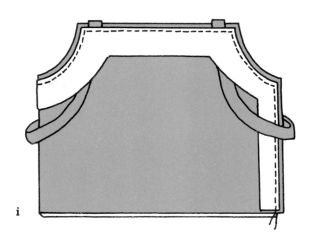

i

j Right-hand side seam and facing can be stitched in one operation.

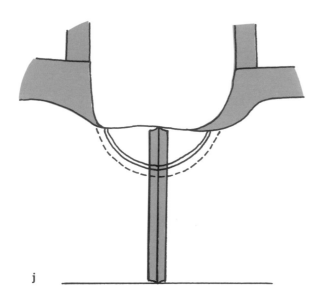

j

k Add buttons and buttonholes as illustrated. If you cannot face doing buttonholes there are poppers available that look exactly like buttons when attached to a garment. They are particularly useful on thick or difficult fabrics.

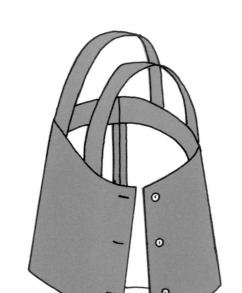

k

19. Strap fastening

Duffel coat

a Place fabric and lining right sides together. Stitch round edges, leaving an opening to turn strap to right side. Trim and clip seams.

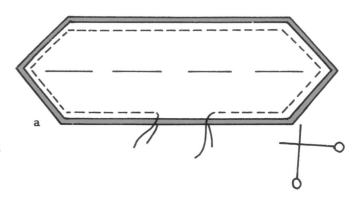

a

b Turn flap to right side and handstitch opening.

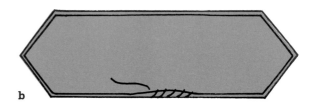

b

c Make buttonholes at both ends of strap.

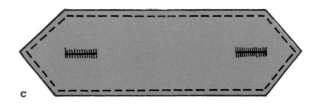

c

20. Reinforced facing

21. Gathering

Wrapover skirt

a Neaten front edges of wrap and attach a 6 cm width of bonded adhesive webbing (as used for turning hems) to each one.

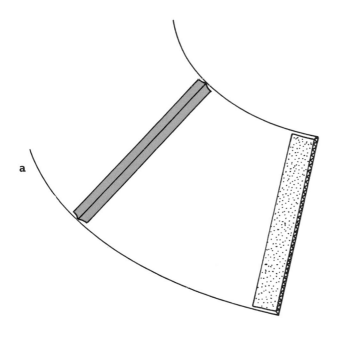

b Turn reinforced parts of wrapover to inside of skirt and press into place.

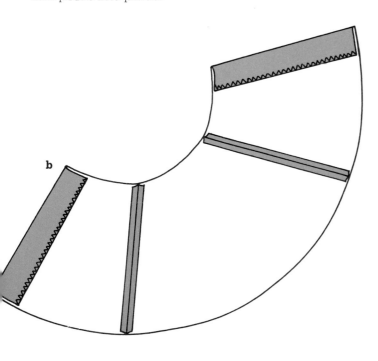

Gathering a skirt (or trousers) to fit a bodice

a Gather top edge of skirt in four equal quarters, *not* as a continous line of stitching. This makes for easier positioning to bodice.

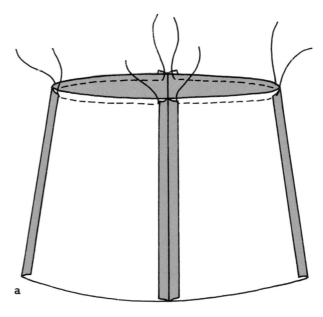

b Pin bodice to gathered edge, carefully placing quarter positions to side seams, centre front and centre back. Stitch into position and neaten seam edges.

Note For a slighly tighter-fitting garment you can machine elastic to this seam allowance.

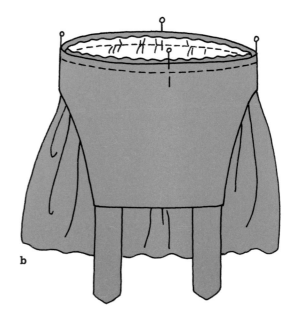

139

22. Contrast bands

This is a technique that is not only decorative, but also very useful if you are short of fabric or want to make a repair.

a Decide where you want to position the contrast bands.

b When you cut through your pattern *remember to add a seam allowance* to both cut edges for stitching the pieces together again.

c Stitch contrast pieces to garment one at a time, until you have a complete garment piece.

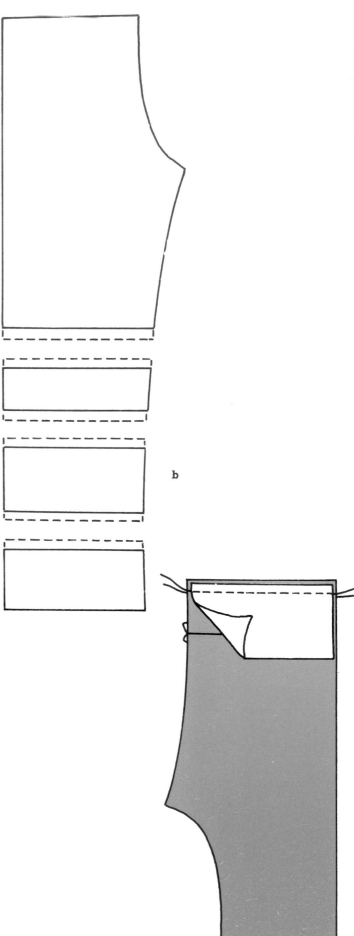

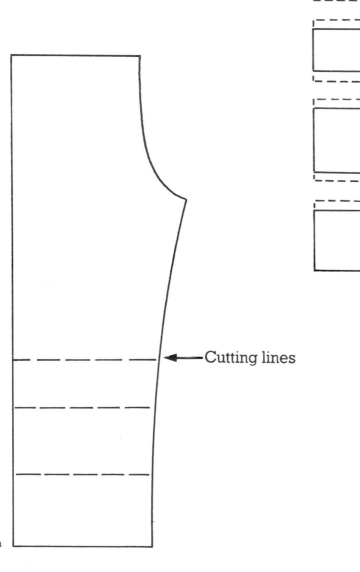

◄——Cutting lines

23. Stitch and turn cased linings

Rompers and shorts

a Make up garment in main fabric and lining. Stitch straps to front bib. Tuck straps down between garment and lining, right sides together, and stitch around top edge, as illustrated. Stitch elastic across top back of rompers for a snug fit.

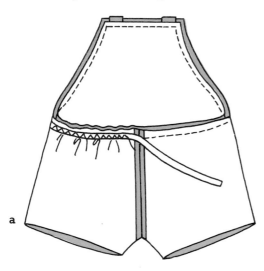

b Turn lining to inside, pushing it down into legs. Stitch the two fabrics together at bottom of legs, then turn and stitch a hem through which elastic can be threaded.

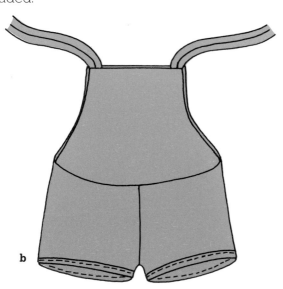

Note The use of 'webbed' elastic will give a shirred effect to the legs.

Suntop

c Make up bodice and lining. Make straps and stitch to bodice (see technique 17).

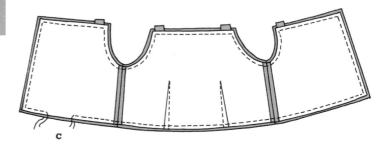

d Place lining and bodice right sides together and stitch all round edges, leaving a small opening to push top through to right side. Close opening with handstitching.

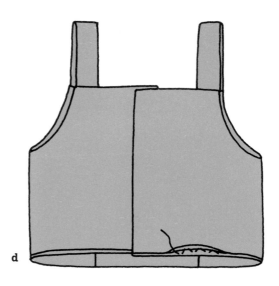

141

24. Wrapover bodice

a Make long tie ends from matching or contrast fabric. No pattern is given for this, so ensure that the ties are long enough to reach from the sides of the waist and make a satisfactory bow at the back (see strap-making technique on page 135). Stitch ties to right side of each wrapover.

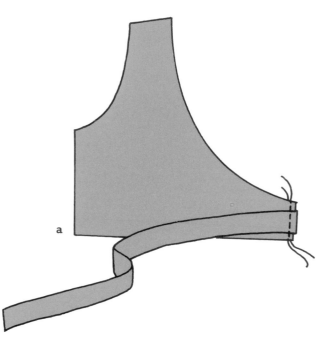

b With right sides together and ties tucked inside, place lining on wrapovers. Stitch round front curved edge, across tie seam and along waistline.

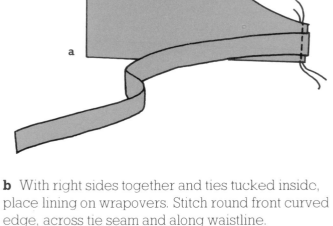

c Trim and clip seams. Turn wrapovers to right side and stitch to front bodice at shoulders, round armholes and down side seams, leaving enough seam allowance at waistline for skirt to be attached.

d If you prefer, the wrapovers can be buttoned at either side and the ties can be stitched into the side seams.

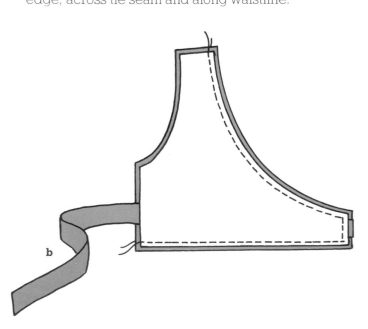

25. Frilling

A wide variety of ready-made frilling is available and can save a lot of work and calculation. However, it is often more practical to make your own frilling and you can do this in two ways.

Single thickness

a Cut a bias strip at least *twice* the finished length you require, and allow sufficient width for hemming outside edge. (If you prefer, you may use zig-zag stitch to neaten the edge.)

a

Double thickness

b Cut a bias strip *twice* the finished length and width you require. Fold it in half lengthways, wrong sides together, and gather along raw edges to required length.

The optimum amount of frilling depends on the type of fabric being used. Experiment on a small piece first and then you can accurately calculate your requirement. As a very rough guide, the frilling strip should be at least twice as long as you require.

b

Pleating

c This requires a bias strip *three* times longer than the finished length required and may be done with either single or double fabric.

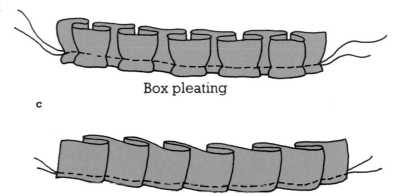

Box pleating

c

Knife pleating

Frilled neckline with binding

d Stitch frilling to neckline with centre back seam folded to inside of garment. Bind neckline in fabric to match garment (see technique 1).

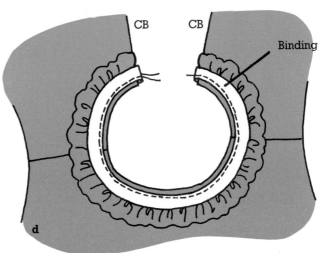

CB   CB

Binding

d

e Finished neck trim should lie flat like this.

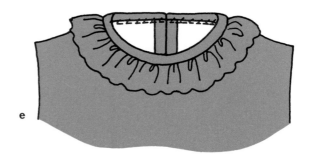

e

Frilled neckline with facing

f If using a facing, stitch frilling to neckline up to centre back only. Place facing on garment and stitch round neckline and down facing on centre back seamline. Trim and clip seam. Turn facing to inside of garment.

i Place lining on yoke, right sides together, enclosing frilling, and stitch round neckline and down front edges. Clip and trim seams. Turn yoke to right side.

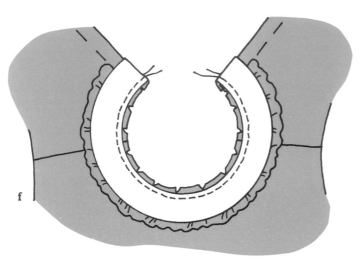

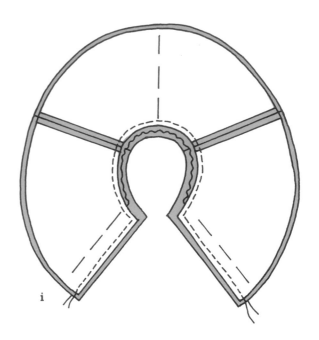

g Finished neck trim should stand upright like this.

j Neaten curved edges of shoulder frills, and trim with lace, if required. Gather straight edges and stitch a frill to each armhole edge of yoke, distributing gathers evenly on both sides of shoulder seams. Make buttonholes and add buttons to yoke (see technique 18).

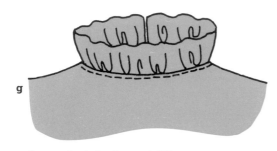

Long-sleeved nightdress frilling

h Stitch shoulder seams of top yoke and also lining yoke. Neaten curved edge of neckline frilling and trim with lace, if required. Gather straight edge and stitch to neck edge of main fabric, right sides together, up to centre front line.

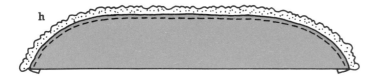

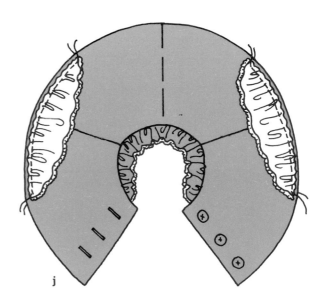

k Stitch front of nightdress to fronts of sleeves. Stitch back of nightdress to back of sleeves.

m Stitch gathered nightdress to yoke. (Tack centre front buttoned wrap at bottom before doing this.)

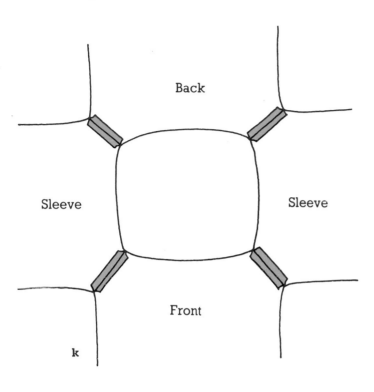

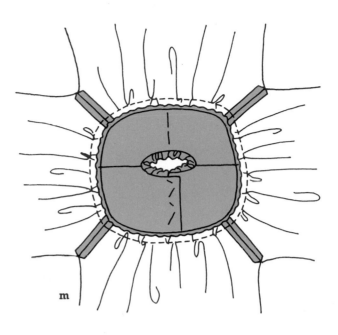

l Using gathering method from technique 21, use four separate threads to gather nightdress to fit yoke, matching sleeve line positions as in pattern instructions.

n Stitch side seams and sleeve seams in one operation. Neaten and gather bottom of sleeves as described in technique 7. Lace trimming may be added to match the frills.

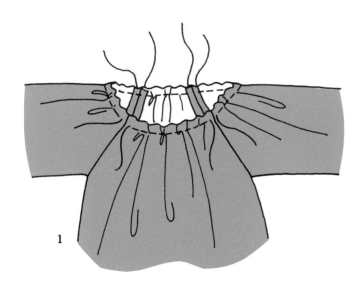

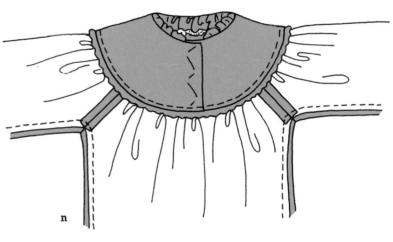

26. Double yoke

There are many sewing techniques to attach a double yoke to a garment. The illustrations here show one method that can be successfully used for this purpose.

a Attach collar to neck edge from centre front to centre front.

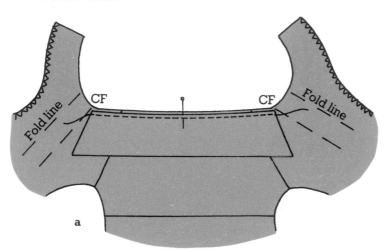

b Fold back front facings and stitch them to back yoke at shoulder seams. Matching centre back points, stitch full neck facing to the neckline, enclosing collar. Trim and clip seam.

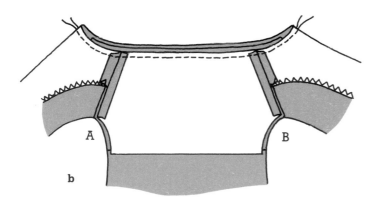

c Turn facing (which now includes lining yoke) to inside of garment and press a hem on raw edge of lining yoke. Stitch to back yoke seam and also stitch shoulder seams to garment.

This stitching can be done by machine if you stitch in the 'ditch' of outer seam line.

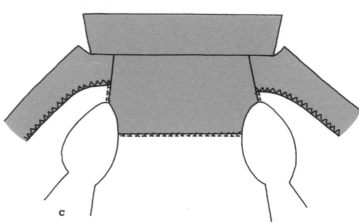

Motifs

Often a plain garment can be made more attractive by adding a decorative touch in the form of a 'picture'. Motifs can be expensive to buy, so you can save money and be original if you make up your own ideas. To get you started, the following pages contain some simple outlines that you can trace off and apply to your garment.

There are three main ways of attaching motifs.

1 You can buy a special tracing paper with an adhesive backing.

a Trace the design on to the paper and cut it out. Using a damp cloth and a fairly hot iron, press the design on to the *wrong* side of the motif fabric.

b Peel away the paper, carefully position the motif on the garment, and use a damp cloth and hot iron to fix permanently in place.

This type of paper comes with full instructions, but do remember that the motif fabric *must* be colourfast and should ideally be similar to the fabric used for the garment.

2 Trace the motifs on thin paper and use it as a pattern to cut your fabric. Use little spots of adhesive webbing to position the motif on the garment or tack it into place. Satin stitch round the edges by hand, or use a close zig-zag or embroidery stitch on your sewing maching to secure the motif.

3 You can use ordinary tissue paper to trace the motifs. Pin the tracing to the garment, tack into position and then embroider round the outline. This method avoids the use of motif fabric, but can look very attractive if you use different colours of embroidery thread. Tear the tissue paper away once you have completed the work.

You can make these motifs in odd scraps of fabric, perhaps using different colours for the fish's fins and a sequin for the eye. The balloon strings can be embroidered or made of ribbon.

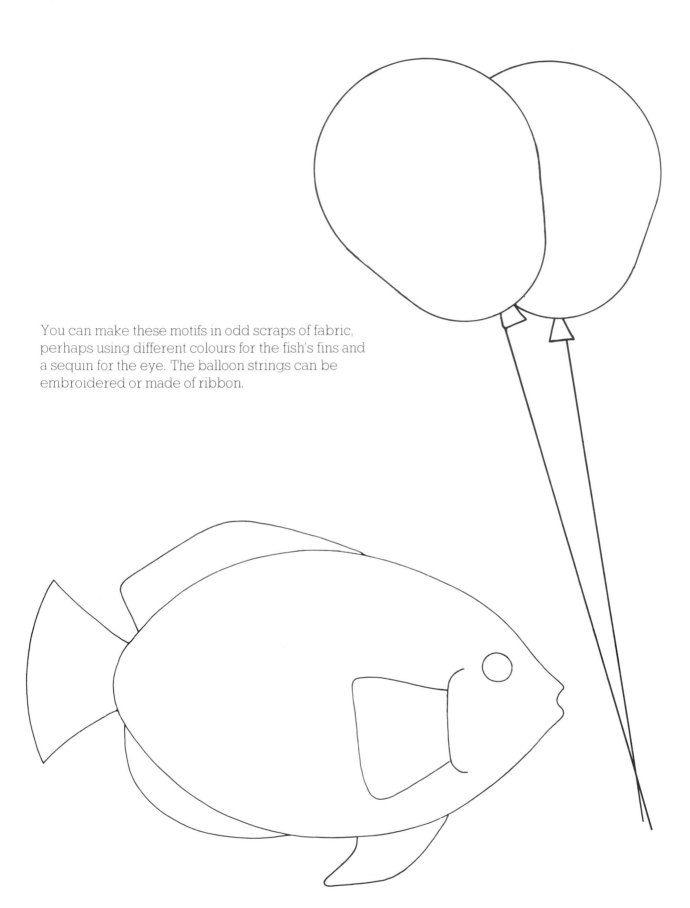

If you have a scrap of fur fabric, you can make a very strokable bunny. Give it a pink button for an eye.

Try picking out the kite
tails in different colours
of fabric or embroidery
thread.

The markings on the sea-horse and alligator could be embroidered in a different colour from the main outline to add an interesting texture.

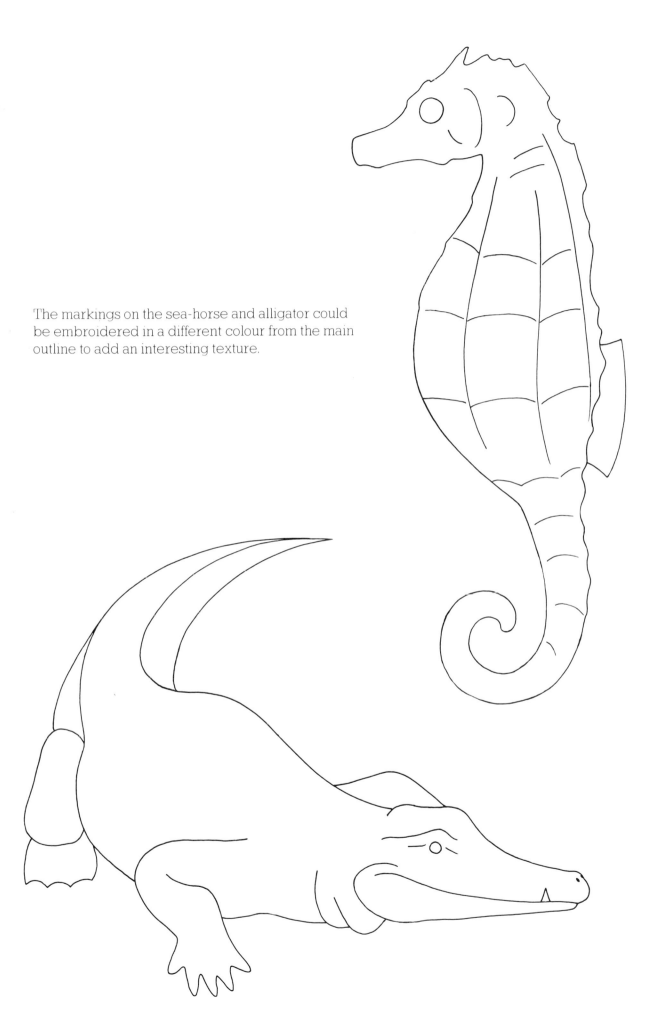

Fabric glossary

Choosing fabric

The range of fabrics available today is so varied and exciting that it is easy to get carried away with enthusiasm and not take careful account of how it will make up as a garment, and how it will wash and wear. There are several basic points to remember.

• As children's garments are often made from very small pattern pieces, you must be careful to avoid patterned fabric that has wide gaps between repeats in the design. (Think of the matching that some wallpapers need!)

• Check the direction of any design to see if the fabric must be cut one way only. This applies not only to the length of the fabric, but also across the width where things like flowers with stems can be all facing in one direction.

• Checked fabrics have always posed great difficulties in dressmaking. The first thing you must do is to fold the fabric in half lengthways and ensure that the checks lie directly over each other at the selvedges. Perfect alignment means that the fabric has been woven, knitted or printed without going off the straight. If the checks do not align at the selvedges you will have considerable matching difficulty with all sections of the garment. A partial solution could be to make parts of the garment on the crossway grain so that the unmatched checks will not show up so obviously.

• One of the biggest problems with stripes and checks occurs when it is not possible to fold the fabric and *mirror* the design exactly underneath, so that two sections, such as sleeves, cannot be cut together as mirrored opposites. I am often tempted to buy this type of fabric but find it not only difficult and wasteful to cut mirrored pieces, but absolutely impossible. The only solution is to take care when buying, and test for folding in the shop.

• Cost will be an important factor in the type of fabric that you buy, but it is false economy if the fabric you buy shrinks when washed, or the colour runs. Fabrics made of 100 per cent natural fibres can be prone to shrinkage, so if you are in any doubt, wash your material before cutting out.

• One thing that is certain about children's clothes is that they will require constant washing, so choose strong, hard-wearing materials, and avoid soft open weaves. Knitted fabrics give excellent wear, and because they are able to stretch slightly, they are very comfortable and the seams do not split with active wear.

• Easy-care fabrics, often a mixture of fibres, such as cotton and polyester, will mean less ironing. This is a useful point to remember, as very small clothes can be difficult to iron.

Some of the fabrics you can expect to find are included in the following list.

Barathea
WOVEN

This was orginally a close woven silk used in tie-making. It was later made from a silk and worsted wool mixture, and is now made entirely from worsted wool. It makes very good suits, blazers, trousers and coats.

Batiste
WOVEN

A fine soft cotton now made with a percentage of polyester. (Some 100 per cent polyester batistes are also available.) It is very useful for lining bodices and yokes because of its fineness, and can also be used for shirts, blouses, underslips and nightwear.

Bedford cord

WOVEN

This is made from any yarn, but is identified by a lengthways ribbed effect. Used for heavy duty wear, such as riding breeches, winter coats and warm trousers.

Blanket cloth

WOVEN

Originally made for covering beds, this is a thick, non-fraying fabric made from wool or a mixture of fibres. Often available as a reversible material, it is suitable for capes and duffel coats. It is sometimes produced with a napped finish like velvet.

Blazer cloth

WOVEN

Warm and lightweight, this is available in pure wool and in mixed fibres. A type of flannel that is good for children's coats.

Brocade

WOVEN

Originally a heavy silk, but now a name for any fabric that has a raised woven pattern and a simple weave for the background. It is often used for bridal and bridesmaid dresses, and when made as curtain fabric, can be used for fancy dress costume, as suggested on page 104.

Broderie anglais

WOVEN

This is an embroidered fabric (usually cotton) that has small holes in the motifs. Imitation broderie anglais is available, but the embroidery does not incorporate the small holes, which identify the real thing.

Brushed acrilan

KNITTED

Ideal for babies' sleeping bags and for dressing-gowns, this thick, light fabric comes in a variety of pretty shades. It must be used with great care because it is very flammable. The fabric is usually acrylic fibre on a jersey backing and normally has a nap finish, which means cutting in one direction only.

Brushed cotton

WOVEN

This is 100 per cent cotton, available in plain colours or prints. The brushing process, applied to the right side of the fabric, gives it warmth. Use it for dresses, blouses and skirts, but be aware that it creases and will require careful ironing.

Brushed nylon

KNITTED JERSEY

Like brushed cotton, the right side of this fabric has a brushed finish for warmth. It washes well and requires no ironing.

Calico

WOVEN

Creases very easily, but is strong and washes and wears well. It is usually 100 per cent cotton, but can be mixed with synthetic fibres.

Cambric

WOVEN

First made in Cambrai, France, from a linen yarn, this fabric is now usually 100 per cent cotton of a very fine quality.

Cheesecloth

WOVEN

This loose woven cotton fabric has a wrinkled appearance. If 100 per cent cotton, it is not hardwearing, but the addition of synthetic fibres improves both the wear and washability.

Chiffon

WOVEN

This is a very delicate fabric woven from highly twisted yarn, which makes the edges roll after cutting out. Can be made from nylon, polyester and pure silk, and drapes beautifully.

Clydella

WOVEN

A trade name for a soft, plain or print mixture of cotton and wool.

Corduroy

WOVEN

Usually made in cotton, but can be a mixture of fibres. Firm to handle and with long, velvety ribs running down the length of the fabric. Corduroy must be cut in one direction only to avoid shading.

Denim

WOVEN

Traditionally blue, but now a fashion fabric in many shades. Twill weave cotton or polyester cotton are most widely available. Denim washes and wears well, but will crease in wear. A stretch variety can now be bought, which is especially useful for tight jeans.

154

Flannel

WOVEN

This is loosely woven wool, or a mixture of wool and other fibres. It wears well and does not fray easily, so is therefore useful for many garments, such as trousers, blazers and coats.

Fur fabric

This is usually an acrylic pile on a firm jersey or woven backing. For cutting, it must be treated as real fur. Take careful note of the direction of the pile and mark the pattern on the wrong side of the material. Seam edges must have the pile clipped away before stitching. Any pile caught in the seam should be teazed out with a pin after stitching. This is a useful fabric for trimming and for soft toys.

Gaberdine

WOVEN

The twill weave of this cloth makes it water repellent, and it is also sometimes proofed for raincoats. Mixed fibre fabrics, and 100 per cent synthetic fabrics, such as Trevira, are excellent when produced with the gaberdine look.

Gingham

WOVEN

This is very strong and hard-wearing 100 per cent cotton, or a cotton mixture. Often produced in checks or stripes, it is widely used for children's blouses, shirts and school dresses.

Jersey

KNITTED

This is a name for any fabric that is knitted rather than woven. It can be made from almost any fibre or mixture of fibres.

Lawn

WOVEN

This is a very soft and delicate cotton fabric, also available as a mixture of cotton and synthetic fibres. It is often used for baby clothes, and many famous trade names (including Liberty) use this fabric for blouses, dresses and shirts.

Needlecord

WOVEN

This is a fine-ribbed version of corduroy, which is hard-wearing and usually washable. It is normally made of cotton, but can be made with a percentage of synthetic fibres. It must always be cut in one direction to avoid shading.

Organdie

WOVEN

Made from very fine yarn to give a transparent effect, organdie is usually stiffened and has a glazed finish. Use it for collars, pinafores, special dresses and delicate blouses.

Piqué

WOVEN

This is a hard-wearing cotton or synthetic fabric, which is very similar to needlecord in that it is woven with a close rib. Use it for making shirts, trousers, dungarees, collars and cuffs.

Poplin

WOVEN

This is a plain cotton or synthetic fabric with a characteristic shine on the right side. It is very hard-wearing and often used for pockets. As it is difficult to hand sew, be careful with hems, which can look better machined.

PVC

This is usually made from cotton which has been coated with polyvinyl chloride to make it shiny and waterproof. It is a very useful fabric for bibs, overalls, aprons and rain capes. A little oil on the machine needle, helps the stitching, and a fine sprinkling of talcum powder can help the fabric glide under the machine foot if you are stitching from the right side. Try to use bound edges to avoid hems.

Quilted fabric

WOVEN OR KNITTED

Any fabric can be quilted to give warmth and effect. Terylene wadding is sandwiched between the main fabric and the backing fabric (which forms the lining) and then machined together in a geometric pattern to form one fabric. Use it for complete garments, or for sections of a garment as decoration.

Reversible fabric

Many fabrics can be used on both sides, which can look very attractive if you want to create a trimmed effect without buying additional fabric. Some reversible fabrics are made from two layers of cloth of different colours or design, stitched, or permanently stuck, together. These fabrics are excellent on such garments as capes or duffel coats when you do not wish to use a lining. Edges should be bound.

Satin

WOVEN

This word describes a type of weave as well as a type of fabric. It always has a smooth, lustrous surface and is made from a continuous filament thread such as pure silk or nylon. Take care to avoid iron marks when pressing.

Seersucker

WOVEN

This is usually cotton, or a cotton mixture, which washes well and needs no ironing. It is characterized by its bubbly, uneven surface.

Silk

WOVEN

An expensive but very beautiful fabric that is not difficult to handle. Try to use silk thread and always test for ironing on small pieces.

Stretch jersey

KNITTED

This is a two-way stretch fabric available in many weights and types, made from polyester, cotton and other fibres. It is suitable for trousers, sports wear, and many other garments, but the seams must stretch with the fabric so the right thread must be used. Ideally, it should be sewn on a machine with a small zig-zag or stretch stitch facility. Ball point or perfect-stitch needles can also help in the handling.

Towelling

WOVEN

This fabric, often called terry towelling, is made from thick cotton with close loops, and is ideal for beach robes and dressing-gowns. It is often possible to make children's garments more cheaply, and in better quality towelling if you use household towels rather than buy from a roll.

Stretch towelling, which is jersey backed, is ideal for beach wear, anoraks and shorts, but is usually available only in very wide widths.

Velour jersey

KNITTED

This is usually made from acrylic fibre with a velvet pile running in one direction on the right side. Not often hard-wearing, but very attractive in glowing colours, and with a stretch quality that allows you to make garments without zips or openings to get them on. Cut in the same way as velvet. Making up must be done with a small zig-zag or stretch stitch, which will give with the fabric.

Velvet

WOVEN

A sophisticated pile fabric (sometimes called street velvet), which was originally made in 100 per cent cotton with the velvet surface cut after weaving. Velvet is now available with mixed fibres, but I recommend only 100 per cent cotton velvet for satisfactory home dressmaking. It must be cut in one direction only, the decision being made after you have assessed which way you prefer. You will find the colour stronger when the pile goes *upwards* on the garment.

Velveteen

WOVEN

This is a very short pile cotton velvet, highly recommended for children's clothes because it handles and washes more easily than true velvet. It must be cut in one direction.

Viyella

WOVEN

Like Clydella, Viyella is a trade name, but often used to describe any soft, warm mixture of wool and cotton. It can be plain or printed.

Winceyette

WOVEN

This is a type of brushed cotton that wears and washes well, but should only be bought if flame-proofed by the manufacturer. Always ask about this when buying your material; the small additional cost is more than offset by the safety factor.

Wool

WOVEN OR KNITTED

This is a traditional and beautiful fabric, but if 100 per cent pure wool, it is expensive. Some wool mixtures feel and handle like the real thing, but have the added bonus of crease resistance, strength, shape retention and washability. Ask about these qualities when you are buying.

Fabric Care

The International Textile Care Labelling Code is a system of symbol labelling designed to standardize care instructions and to provide consumers with the guidance necessary to ensure that they obtain maximum satisfaction and use from the textile articles they buy.

There are ten possible washing processes that, with a few minor exceptions, cover the whole range of known washable fabrics. Since washing practices differ it is unlikely that all processes will be used in every country or that all of those used will be required at each wash.

	Examples of application	Benefits
MACHINE | **HAND WASH** 95° | Very hot to boil, maximum wash | Hand-hot or boil Spin or wring	White cotton and linen articles without special finishes	Ensures whiteness and stain removal
2 **MACHINE** | **HAND WASH** 60° | Hot, maximum wash | Hand-hot Spin or wring	Cotton, linen or viscose articles without special finishes where colours are fast at 60°C	Maintains colours
3 **MACHINE** | **HAND WASH** 60° | Hot, medium wash | Hand-hot Cold rinse. Short spin or drip-dry	White nylon; white polyester/cotton mixtures	Prolongs whiteness — minimizes creasing
4 **MACHINE** | **HAND WASH** 50° | Hand-hot, medium wash | Hand-hot Cold rinse. Short spin or drip dry	Coloured nylon; polyester; cotton and viscose articles with special finishes; acrylic/cotton mixtures; coloured polyester/cotton mixtures	Safeguards colour & finish — minimizes creasing
MACHINE | **HAND WASH** 40° | Warm, maximum wash | Warm Spin or wring	Cotton, linen or viscose articles where colours are fast at 40°C, but not at 60°C	Safeguards the colour fastness
6 **MACHINE** | **HAND WASH** 40° | Warm, minimum wash | Warm Cold rinse. Short spin. Do not wring	Acrylics; acetate and triacetate, including mixtures with wool; polyester/wool blends	Preserves colour & shape — minimizes creasing
MACHINE | **HAND WASH** 40° | Warm, minimum wash | Warm, Do not rub Spin. Do not hand wring	Wool, including blankets and wool mixtures with cotton or viscose; silk	Keeps colour, size and handle
8 **MACHINE** | **HAND WASH** 30° | Cool, minimum wash | Cool Cold rinse. Short spin. Do not wring	Silk and printed acetate fabrics with colours not fast at 40°C	Prevents colour loss
9 **MACHINE** | **HAND WASH** 95° | Very hot to boil, minimum wash | Hand-hot or boil Drip-dry	Cotton articles with special finishes capable of being boiled but requiring drip drying	Prolongs whiteness, retains special crease resistant finish
HAND WASH	Articles which must not be machine washed. Details will vary because garment manufacturers put their own written instructions on this label	
	Do not wash	

Index